# YOUR NEIGHBOR'S HYMNAL

# Your Neighbor's Hymnal

What Popular Music Teaches Us
about Faith, Hope, and Love

JEFFREY F. KEUSS

CASCADE *Books* · Eugene, Oregon

Your Neighbor's Hymnal
What Popular Music Teaches Us about Faith, Hope, and Love

Cascade Books
An Imprint of Wipf and Stock Publishers
199 W. 8th Ave., Suite 3
Eugene, OR 97401

www.wipfandstock.com

ISBN 13: 978-1-60899-369-7

*Cataloging-in-Publication data:*

Keuss, Jeffrey F.

    Your neighbor's hymnal : what popular music teaches us about faith, hope, and love / Jeffrey F. Keuss

    x + 140 p. ; 23 cm. Includes bibliographical references and index.

    ISBN 13: 978-1-60899-369-7

    1. Popular music—Religious aspects—Christianity. I. Title.

BV1534.8 K35 2011

Manufactured in the U.S.A.

For my band of brothers: Mike, Kurt, Stu, Jeff, and Tom.

You have taken Jake and Elwood Blues' mantra

"We are on a mission from God"

to redeeming heights and depths.


Psalm 73: 25, 26

# Contents

# Acknowledgments

How about a cheer for all those bad girls
and all the boys
that play that rock and roll
they love it
like you love Jesus
it does the same thing
to their souls . . .

**—Tom Petty and the Heartbreakers,
"Have Love Will Travel"**

I N 2002, AFTER LOSING some traction and experiencing some artistic and critical misfires, Tom Petty and the Heartbreakers released an album entitled *The Last DJ* that took the recording industry to task for pandering to quick-fix hits and for its unwillingness to work with bands artistically to develop in-depth and critical excellence. One of the songs on the album was "Have Love Will Travel," a bit of a love song to fans who seek out great music and the bands that produce it. When Petty performs this song live in concert, the third verse printed above elicits a roar from the audience.

In many ways, this book is a shout out to the bad girls and rock-and-roll boys who love pop music with fierceness akin to a Southern revival meeting and the places that serve as their cathedrals—those great music stores like Easy Street Records, Sonic Boom, and Cellophane Square in Seattle, Lost in Music and Fopp in Glasgow's West End, and many others that think pop music matters to the very core of our being. My thanks to countless music lovers over the years who challenged me to listen to new bands, went to concerts with me, lamented the deaths of great artists, and went with me to midnight release parties. Part of this book found its genesis in conversations with the Kindlings Muse community on Monday nights at Hales Ales and Pub in Fremont where we wrestled with the intersection of faith and culture in ways that were at turns profound, hilarious, somber, and transcendent. I owe them a great debt for putting up with my ever-wandering brain but always inviting me back for another conversation. Some of this book began during my time as a pastor in the early 1990s at a ragtag church plant in downtown Seattle called Church at the Center, which met in a movie theater under the shadow of Seattle's Space Needle. Some of the songs in this collection were new back in those days and were part of the worship life in that community. The Church at the Center family gave me insight into how powerful a pop song can be to people, how close to the heart and even how painful it can be when bound to broken relationships and lost dreams. Even though that congregation ceases to be, I pray that my musings honor that congregation and the vision they had for the sacred and secular to hang out in worship together. My thanks to Amy Whitley, Erin Rodenbiker, and Kristi Kiger for reviewing early versions of this book. And a special thanks to my wife, Diana, whose editorial eye gave me faith and hope in this project and whose heart continues to give me reason to believe that a section called "love" could be written not only in words but in life.

Lastly, I commit this book to you, dear reader and listener. We hear from Scripture that transformational interpretation is a divine mingling together of insights that arises sometimes from the text itself (e.g., 2 Tim. 3:17), sometimes from trusting the human authors of Scripture (e.g., 2 Pet. 1:21), and sometimes, at least by implication, from those who are contemporary readers of Scripture (e.g., Luke 24:49), which means people like you and me. Similarly, I pray that as you listen anew to these songs and others, that you would find blessing in the songs themselves, the singers and songwriters, and trust yourself as readers and listeners to find new ways to find faith, hope, and love.

# 1

# Introduction

I can't imagine anything but music that could have brought about this alchemy. Maybe it's because music is about as physical as it gets: your essential rhythm is your heartbeat, your essential sound, the breath. We're walking temples of noise, and when you add tender hearts to this mix, it somehow lets us meet in places we couldn't get to any other way.

**—Anne Lamott**[1]


"And what is the saint doing in the forest?" asked Zarathustra. The saint answered: "I make songs and sing them; and when I make songs, I laugh, cry, and hum: thus do I praise God. With singing, crying, laughing, and humming do I praise the God who is my God."

**—Friedrich Nietzsche**[2]


## WHY SHOULD THE DEVIL HAVE ALL THE GOOD MUSIC?

CHRISTMAS MORNING, 1977. I reached under the Christmas tree in my parent's house and unwrapped a gift that would change everything:

1. Lamott, *Traveling Mercies*, 67.
2. Nietzsche, *Thus Spoke Zarathustra*, Prologue, sec. 2 (p. 124).

1

a plastic, beige Sears cassette player with six D cell batteries and a cassette tape of Fleetwood Mac's 1977 release, *Rumours*. I unwrapped the cellophane, put the tape into the player, placed the small plastic earbuds into my ears, and hit the play button. Lindsey Buckingham's jangly opening chords slowly grew from his guitar—starting softly and building like a rushing train exploding from a tunnel, colliding with Mic Fleetwood's drums and Stevie Nick's vocals in the opener, "Second Hand News." As the anxiety of Buckingham's harmony vocals blended and weaved with the raw assurance of Stevie Nicks' melody, I knew in ways I didn't have language for that something was going on here that was magical. I was twelve years old and had a number of great gifts from Christmases past but this was something different—voices pushing against instruments and crashing into a mosaic that was both frustrated and solemn. In three minutes it was over, and the next song picked up the silence and painted a new canvas, this time a ballad titled "Dreams," which was completely different with Christine McVie's softer delivery, yet strangely familiar with the preceding track. *Rumours* would go on to sell over forty million albums worldwide and continues to have multiple afterlives, from being used in graduation ceremonies and dating mix tapes for decades to the Clinton presidential campaign and various commercials for everything from cars to real estate. But for a twelve-year-old boy it was the closest thing to transcendence I had ever heard. These were songs about pain, sex, loss, anger, hope, and love that I didn't understand, but the emotion coupled with the music cut a furrow in my soul in the way an iron plow cuts into hardpan and transforms it into life-giving soil. Three decades later the songs on *Rumours* can bring me back to points in my life where the same song encountered all the emotions I didn't understand at twelve but have since lived through in all the pain and joy that a life will offer. As Cath Carroll notes in her book on the rise and fall of Fleetwood Mac and the making of the *Rumours* album, this was an album that fully acknowledged that "music was the common language of youth culture" and "speaks of the golden California days before irony usurped innocence, and before punk rock came along and tried to make rock music feel old and stupid."[3] What I was discovering through pop music was truly a language that over the years would identify the highs and lows of life in ways that few things ever would, provid a connection with other people who

---

3. Carroll, *Never Break the Chain*, 10.

thought in terms of melodies and lyrics more than doctrines and platitudes, and harken back to what was hoped and dreamed for in life when
the prevailing culture seemed bent on destruction, despair, and nihilism.
While this early introduction to the power of pop music would grow over
the next few years, I would eventually become tempted to doubt it and
walk away for a time. As I would come to find out, Evangelicalism in the
early 1980s was not a bilingual culture, and a jealous one at that.

Probably the biggest challenge to how and why I listen to music has
come through my embracing of evangelical Christianity in high school
and the uneasy place so-called secular pop music holds within that subculture. In the parachurch ministries in which I found community and
fellowship I also found a strange relationship with music. There was no
written listening guides to what was considered pagan, sinful, sanctified,
or blessed, but one thing was for certain: if you wanted to be safe, you
were to trust the record label more than the artist or the musical content.
Christian bookstores in those days sold records and cassette tapes on labels such as Word, Sparrow, and Reunion, and these were akin to hothouse
flowers—they could only live and flourish in these bookstores (there was
no Internet remember) and were therefore strangely alternative. These
labels were headed by Christians, I was told, and therefore "safe"—by
Christian record executive priests who took the common elements of a
recording artist and the formulations of the current secular musical tastes
and transubstantiated them into something known as "Contemporary
Christian Music" (otherwise known as CCM). These sanctified records
and tapes were deemed safe for consumption without any need for critical
reflection or discernment. While no one expressly forced me to burn my
untransubstantiated record albums by artists such as the Beatles, Rush,
Jackson Browne, ABBA, Bob Dylan, and Simon and Garfunkel, I was told
on a number of occasions to get rid of them in favor of something that
had more direct references to faith—songs that contained words such
as "Jesus," "faith," and "hope" and told stories aligned with those found
in Scripture. The fact that Scripture itself frames its starting place as the
engagement with God intertwining with the down-and-dirty of real life
that, upon reflection and divine inspiration, has become the canon that
has framed the community of Christian faith, didn't seem to matter in the
world of CCM in the 1970s and 1980s. All of this came to a head for me
in the late 80s when, as part of my work as a media relations manager for a
large Christian ministry in the Pacific Northwest, I travelled to a number

of National Religious Broadcasting (NRB) regional meetings as well as the Gospel Music Association's (GMA) equivalent to the Grammys: the Dove Awards. I was meeting with owners of Christian radio stations as well as record executives from CCM labels and the artists they represented. As much as I heard words like "Jesus," "faith," and "hope" in many of the songs in that era, I also saw money, envy, fear, celebrity, and the quest for fame as much as I witnessed in other mass media. I was shocked, as many people are, to see that what is behind the big curtain of CCM are still broken and wounded people—many with sincere hearts and a desire for art to transcend the mundane and trivial, to be sure. At the GMA's 1990 Dove Awards I was seated in a large auditorium in Nashville at the beginning of a singer-songwriter showcase where recording executives were invited to hear the "next big thing" as up-and-coming CCM artists offered up their hearts and voices for the chance to land a recording contract. During the sound check for one artist I heard something strangely familiar. Slowly pulsing out of the speakers was a familiar guitar riff that built with energy and was then joined by drums and bass that took me back to Christmas morning in 1977. To warm up, this artist was covering Fleetwood Mac's "Don't Stop (Thinking about Tomorrow)," a big single off the *Rumours* album. I can't even begin to explain this clash of cultures as I looked around at the other recording executives who, upon recognizing the song, let smiles creep across their faces and started tapping their loafers to the beat. The artist only went through the first verse ("Open your eyes and look at the day / You will see things in a different way") and then told the guy at the soundboard that he was ready for his real set. But the damage was done and I couldn't hear another thing. There was something so false in that moment as those who had been tapping their feet in the room didn't acknowledge that what we all heard was one of the most successful singles in contemporary pop music and, to be frank, a seriously kicking pop riff that hooked us in ways nothing that evening had. To add to that, it communicated a level of longing and angst coupled with a real desire for something beyond the typical and rote ("Don't stop thinking about tomorrow") that all the false optimism pushed through the towering speakers that evening couldn't deal with. For two minutes we heard an honest song, and honesty is what we all want but few can deliver. Six months after that 1990 GMA and Dove awards ceremony I left behind working with the CCM world as a media relations manager to work in hospital administration for three years before going to seminary and then eventually to graduate school to study English literature, cultural theory, and theology. I became involved as a pastor with a church plant in the mid-1990s in downtown Seattle as the grunge movement exploded, and we played music that people—most people, not merely Christians—listened to on a daily basis and not just on a Sunday morning. Bands like REM, Nirvana, Pearl Jam, Toad the Wet Sprocket, as well as Eric Clapton, Jimi Hendrix, and Janis Joplin. In their music we found something that wasn't foreign to what the Christian story was about. As a matter of fact, much of what these so-called secular artists were singing their hearts out for was the same thing everyone I met was crying out for. In their doubts, anger, frustration, and even profanity, as well as hopes and loves, was something that wasn't at odds with the biblical account. In many respects it was the biblical account incarnated and distilled down to a four-minute pop song, and it is for these songs and many others that this book came into being.

Over the years the songs from that first Fleetwood Mac cassette tape and many other songs—some included in this book and many that aren't—have become living things, conversation partners, and at times even embarrassments akin to weird cousins who show up unannounced at Thanksgiving. I have both celebrated and denied their place in my life in the proceeding decades as they fell out of fashion in the face of disco, metal, new romanticism, neo-folk, grunge, and hip-hop and then became "vintage" and therefore cool all over again. Perhaps this has been your story as well, or it has for people you know. But some Christians have distanced themselves from these vital four-minute pop songs in favor of a CCM narrative, and it is my hope for those for whom this is true that they can add some tracks to their music rotation and learn to appreciate the music of our neighbors who might not sit in the pews of our churches but who are asking many of the same questions, who have the same desires, and who hope for the same heaven even if they get there by another soundtrack.

Christian rock pioneer Larry Norman once sang, "Why should the devil have all the good music?" In reality, most of the good music belongs not to the devil but to our neighbor—those that Jesus calls us to love as ourselves. *Your Neighbor's Hymnal* is an opportunity to spend some time reflecting on the wide bandwidth of popular music that our neighbor listens to across the many genres of the FM dial and iTunes catalog—jazz, folk, pop, rock, electronica, and others—and see that our neighbor is not only listening *to* the music that many Christians listen to but also listening *for* the very things that animate the hearts and minds of those sitting in the pews on a Sunday morning. Pop songs have carried the memories, pains, joys, and losses for people even before King David picked up a harp, as every artist over the decades who has covered Leonard Cohen's "Hallelujah" has tried to get at. They are simple tunes with universal messages sung at weddings, high school proms, the birth of children, bar mitzvahs, and the funerals of loved ones. In many ways, it is the simple, disposable nature of pop music that makes it a genre so easy to dismiss as merely entertainment that only distracts us from the true things of life. For many this may indeed be the case. But there is something about pop songs that will cause someone in a car to slow down, turn the radio up just a little bit, and instantly go back to a time in life long since forgotten and now fully remembered in ways novels and movies do not. A song like that is a complete universe that bridges the "then" and the "now" in four minutes and is therefore like a metaphysical splinter in our brain—a tune that we can't shake that awakens parts of us long since departed or a longing that we hope will some day come true. As singer-songwriter Neil Young once said, anything more than three chords is showing off. While many of the songs in *Your Neighbor's Hymnal* certainly push beyond three chords, Young's sentiment remains apropos—there is something in a basic pop song that directly touches a wide breadth of humanity in ways that the most astute and well-researched theological text never will. This is not to disregard so-called serious scholarly work. But traditional scholarship can be a distraction for some in regard to how people's understanding of Jesus' message and ministry can be deepened simply through a four-minute song with predictable hooks.

## THE RISE OF THE SONIC MYSTIC—ON EMPTYING, AWAKING, AND EMBRACING

One of the things I have become acutely aware of is the role pop music plays in how people see and hear the world around them. In his book *How the Beatles Destroyed Rock 'N' Roll: An Alternative History of American Popular Music*, author Elijah Wald seeks to even out the historical imbalances between what the pop eras from the 1890s through the 1960s are best remembered for and how over the years some artists are forgotten as to how influential they were to culture at large. He gives examples like Duke Ellington, who was obviously an important figure in popular music in the 1920s but in his own time was not as popular as Paul Whiteman, the latter a musician who is largely forgotten and overlooked in scholarship. Where Ellington was an innovator, Whiteman took the music and sentimentality of the 1920s and blended it, not in an attempt to change the way that music should be done but to speak to where people were in their time and with music they would be familiar with. Whiteman was a true DJ in the hip-hop sense, blending existing musical forms of symphonic music and jazz that people loved. It was Whiteman who commissioned George Gershwin's "Rhapsody in Blue" and opened up jazz to a popular audience. Whiteman recorded numerous pop standards during his career, with great titles such as "Wang Wang Blues," "Mississippi Mud," and "Hot Lips," and you could hear people whistling his tunes as they walked the streets. Ellington has been preserved and lauded by critics and scholars over the years and therefore preserved for succeeding generations. However, Whiteman made music that was played in dance halls and at celebrations, becoming a star in his own time. But critics and scholars (often rightly) preserve the innovators and geniuses and cease to speak up for the populists, who may not be changing music but are still making the music that speaks to people in their time. These are some of the artists I hope to speak about in the coming pages.

Another factor that has changed how culture consumes and understands popular music is the accelerated changes in technology that have moved music away from being a public event to a private and isolating thing. According to Wald, from the beginning of producing recorded music for home consumption in the form of vinyl records and well into the 1940s, the phonograph record was viewed as revolving sheet music. For example, in a concert review from 1941, Wald notes that the reviewer derides baritone Vaughn Monroe for performing his recorded arrangements before an audience as a live performance, something that would soon become commonplace in the years to come. The change in the way people heard music, from relying on radio, going to concerts, and hearing word-of-mouth acclaim regarding live shows, to the mass production of record albums to be played in the home, gave a greater control to the listener but also engendered solitariness in how people experienced music. "Now, people could put a stack of albums on the hi-fi," notes Wald, "and enjoy a couple hours of uninterrupted music in the comfort of their living rooms."[4] After World War II, the focus of the single household as

4. Wald, *How the Beatles Destroyed Rock 'N' Roll*, 184.

the locus for all consumer activity for marketers, coupled with the growth in televisions entering the home, meant that having to go out and gather with others to enjoy music was becoming more of an option than a necessity. From there it was merely a skip and a jump to the birth of portable transistor radios and car stereos to huge ten-pound boom boxes (at the time considered "portable") and Walkman cassette players, and then to MP3s on iPods, all in a few decades. Now the notion of music stored and played as a physical, analog entity is essentially relegated to a vintage aesthetic preference. As the way consumers interact with recorded music has moved further away from the physical, tactile nature of the record album and reel-to-reel tape into the realm of the "cloud"—stored in digital clarity in the cyber ether that has no limit—the mystical nature of recorded songs seems to be coming into convergence with the nature of sound itself. When people talk about the songs they love, the songs that move them or have deep meaning for them, it is with a transcendent, otherly quality.

To that end, what songs are chart toppers, the what and how of people merely following the herd by buying whatever is hot and happening, or choosing pop culture options because they aren't enlightened to seek after high culture or folk culture options, is not what I wish to discuss here. Rather, I believe that beyond all the discussion of how trashy pop music is, there is still something else going on when a couple falls in love and binds that shared memory to a simple love song they heard—essentially a spiritual engagement as profound as a burning bush, the parting of the Red Sea, or a Damascus road experience. To put it more pointedly, many people listen to pop songs not as a distraction but with a deep hunger for something spiritual and transcendent. It is not out of laziness, nor is it for lack of trying to engage the deep texts of antiquity or for reasoning about the wealth of all collective human wisdom but just not "getting it." No, some people will find answers to life's mysteries at a U2 or Radiohead show in ways that they just will not in the Christian subculture. The consumption of pop music, from wearing concert T-shirts to making mix collections whether on tapes, CDs, or playlists on an iPod, is part of the renewed sense of spirituality that is arising in everyday people around what may seem to be the most mundane of things, in this case pop music. The pulse and crush of sound, whether through sound-cancelling earbuds plugged into an iPod or a subwoofer of a car stereo, is a common occurrence and I argue that the ubiquity of personal MP3 players today is a strong testimony to the fundamental hunger people have in our twenty-first-century culture to forge a life that is free from solidity and certainty and to release into the freedom of sound that is the authentic form of faith. As a metaphor for the search for deep identity in the new millennium, sound is an apt one. We are a generation filled with sound. Our cars pulse with the beat of music pouring from speakers playing the latest hits, our city streets refract these and layer it in the bang and clang of urban movements, and our workplaces blip and ping with computer logon signals and cell phone ringtones. Sound is completely permeable and therefore not restricted by boundary: we can join in with others in singing the chorus of "40" at the end of a U2 concert, adding our voice to those of others.

Physicists have long told us that sound operates as waves that pulse and flow in and through matter. These waves can strike with such force that they can bring matter to the point of shattering. Sound is so powerful and particular, in fact, that everything in the universe has some frequency at which it will vibrate. Whether it is glass, steel, a neutrino subatomic particle in a collider, or the person sitting next to you in the pew, everything has a natural frequency at which it vibrates and this is called a resonant frequency. With enough energy and purity of tone at its resonant frequency, things will vibrate and, with enough force, that resonant frequency will cause everything around to stir, move, and vibrate as well. Think of a wine glass as your finger slides and subtlety sticks along the surface of the glass as you rub it. As you gently circle the rim of the glass, the rubbing imparts energy to the glass molecules and causes them to resonate. The vibrating glass causes air molecules to vibrate at the same frequency causing an inanimate glass to seemingly sing. Moreover, when someone with the sonic force and perfect pitch of opera singer Maria Callas strikes the right note and sustains it the resonant frequency will become so pronounced that it will shatter the glass. Given that at a subatomic level matter is composed of more empty space than solidity, the glass will lose its sense of internal composure as the resonant frequency literarily becomes the dominant identity of the glass and its form. As perceptible as a material object it might have been, the resonant frequency will become all in all and in that instant the glass will give up everything that it was and become so aligned with that pure, sustained note that it will leave its form behind as a wine glass and become at one with sound. What we see is the shattering of glass. What we hear is the sound released, and it is this sound that will continue on into the very reaches of the cosmos striking and stirring frequencies in large and imperceptible ways.

Another point about sound as a metaphor for our lives is that just as sound is a wave in constant motion, we too are things of motion, who are yet to be truly and completely moved and freed. Sound moves into the world without a requirement for return—a note that is released from the throat of a singer remains efficacious and meaningful even without echo or reverberation. To compare our lives to sound is also to remember that we are like distinct frequencies: I have my own identifiable "sonic signature," something that makes me different from another person. Yet, I have the choice of joining with another in such a way that my own voice blends in—or stands out—and the metaphor of sound can be used to communicate either harmony or dissonance in a way that few others can. In this way, the notion of self-as-sound can be used to explore why music is central to every culture on the planet. As people made of sound, it is therefore no surprise that the music our neighbors choose to listen to, to celebrate with, and to mourn with is so close to their hearts, and why music will strike us with the power of our resonant frequency and even a simple pop song, akin to an opera singer shattering a wine glass, will bring us to joy unbridled, torrents of tears, and into the presence of the transcendent God in ways we often cannot fully grasp.

What I am noting as sonic pulsing in resonance frequency is what a musical composition accomplishes and in the mystical tradition of the Christian faith there has long been held the notion that our lives are more evidenced through musical flow and movement than solidity. What it means "to live and move and have our being," as St. Paul reminds us in Acts 17, is that we are beings with lives of flow and movement, rising and falling in relation to our encounter with the Divine.

## PURGATION, ILLUMINATION, AND UNION

This flow of authentic life in relation to the movement of sound mirrors the movement of the mystical experience that is deep in the Christian tradition. For centuries, there has been held the view that to move in the resonant frequency of the living God is to be emptied, awakened, and united in relationship in a continuous threefold movement of purgation, illumination, and union. One key figure who articulated these movements is John Cassian (360–435), in his two major works: *The Institutes* (Latin:

*De institutis coenobiorum*), which deals with the external organization of monastic communities and how communities form; and *The Conferences* (Latin: *Collationes*), which deals with the training of the inner person and the perfection of the heart. These stages of being emptied, awakened, and united in relationship are later articulated by St. John of the Cross (1542–1591), a Spanish Carmelite monk whose key works such as *The Spiritual Canticles* and *The Dark Night of the Soul* exemplify the Gospels accounts of moving from darkness into light in passages such as Matthew 4:1–11, Mark 1:12-13, and Luke 4:1–13.

## Purgation: To Be Emptied So That We Hear Anew

Music encounters us in an act of forgetting and release into new ways of being before it is anything else. Think of a time you first heard a song that grabbed your attention so fully that you stopped what you were doing and lost yourself in it. I remember driving home one evening a few years back when a song came on the radio that not only had I never heard before, but I needed to know what it was because it knocked my socks off. I pulled into a 7-11 parking lot and just sat there till the song was over so I could find out what it was. Before the song had come on, my mind was filled with thoughts about work, picking up some groceries on the way, and what I was going to do with friends that night. All those thoughts just disappeared within the space of a four-minute pop song. I was sitting in a parking lot, my engine running, people coming and going with Slurpees in their hands, but I wasn't there anymore nor was I thinking about time and place at all. I was *in* the song as it moved, collapsed, gained energy, and resolved into the next verse. All the things that seemed so pressing were stalled for a time, a space was opened up in my mind and heart that wasn't there before, and I was just present in the moment. When the song was done, it was as if I awoke into a place not knowing how I got there. For the mystics, this is the movement of purgation or *purgatio*. In this stage a person is brought to awareness that they are not fully present to themselves or to the world around them and something has to give. Think of it as a cold splash of water to the face, tripping over your own feet, or in the case of the sonic mystic, a song that breaks through all the emotional and spiritual static and white noise that clouds our hearts and minds and brings forth that resonant frequency of pure meaning. In the Christian mystical tradition, this is when someone struggles to gain control of "the flesh"—specifically gluttony, lust, and the desire for possessions—in hopes of finding meaning and purpose beyond such things. For the sonic mystic who trolls through the digital downloads on their MP3 player or through the bins of a used record store, it is a similar search for a shock, a slap, a push to move beyond all the crash and bang of meaninglessness and vibrate with the frequency that has moved the planets and stars from the beginning of time. This attempt at emptying that which crowds out meaning, depth, and purpose is the same for both the Christian monk that St. John of the Cross wrote about so long ago as it is for the pop song lovers who ride the bus next to you with headphones embracing their ears. It is important to note that this attempt to break the cycle of mean-inglessness, both for the devout Carmelite monk and the pop music sonic mystic of the twenty-first century, occurs sometimes as an active purging and emptying and sometimes as a passive event that is not planned. In the mystic tradition this is a twin movement of both active and passive purgation. Active purgation or intentional emptying is when the consci-entious monk actively seeks release from that which clouds the *Imago Dei*—the image of God, which is our true identity. The monk is made aware, whether through the counsel of a mentor or through deep prayer and study, that some things about the way we live need to be changed in order to hear God anew. This active purgation can be done through times of silence, working at menial tasks that humble a person, or times of confession and seeking forgiveness to unburden and therefore release those things of the soul that bind the heart and soul. Passive purgation or unintentional emptying of the soul occurs when we are confronted with events, even music, that are surprising, unanticipated, and therefore beyond our control. These moments of passive purgation can make us feel like we have had our pocket picked—not noticing what has happened un-til we reach for what we think is there only to find that it is now gone—had the wind knocked out of us, or have been pulled under while swimming in the surf by a fierce undertow that is unseen yet powerful nonetheless. These moments can occur as revelations of wonder and amazement that bring us joy, like when we meet someone with whom we instantly become smitten, or they can be tragic events that thrust us into suffering or crisis. Whether it be joy or suffering, silence, or the rhythmic beat of a snare drum, high-hat cymbal, and pulsing bass guitar when you are driving—seemingly lost in thought only to have your thoughts jettisoned and your mind opened to something new—it is in this movement of purgation or emptying of the soul that we find that what we have held to be so vital, so important, so foundational to everything we guard as essential, can be released and we become open to the possibility of new ways of being and, more importantly, new or renewed relationships that will bring us there.

## Illumination: When Hearing Becomes Seeing Anew

Once we have been struck by a new song, by the surprising new encounter of love, or the disappointment of loss through crisis, the resources by which we have made sense of life become shifted. The old songs just don't sound the same anymore and we are drawn into the energy, the possibility, and willingness to risk for something beyond that which has been. The "same old, same old" doesn't cut it any longer. It is at this point that the Christian mystics experience illumination, or the *illuminatio* of God, in the form of communities. During this period the monk learned the paths to holiness revealed in the Gospel story and sought to make sense of them in relation to other people. During the *illuminatio* many monks took in visitors and students, and tended the poor as much as their meager resources allowed. For the sonic mystics among us, part of this journey can be seen as we move outside ourselves and deeper into following the artist's career that set them on this journey of discovery—buying CDs in the back catalog, seeking out the live shows, looking into the set lists of past concerts and how artists are changing their music, when they are going into the studio, and what they are heading into next. This seeking after illumination is a seeking for something that is beyond us—that creative spark, the imagination that is aglow with possibilities, the drive to make something new in a world that is derivative. Also, much of this journey of illumination for the sonic mystic is the discovery of the transcendent that shapes the life of the everyday—things like love, caring, compassion, hope, faith, wonder, ecstasy, and awe, which can't be bottled or framed on the wall yet when sung even within a pop song somehow, even for the briefest moment, carry us out of ourselves and bind us to the hearts of others.

For the Carmelite mystic following in the ways of St. John of the Cross, the essential desert island disc that no fanboy of God could go without was the life and teachings of Christ, and in particular what Christ proclaimed as taught the Sermon on the Mount, recounted in the Gospel of Matthew in chapters 5–7. The Christian monk continues his life of humility in the Spirit of God and stretches the self to be formed and re-formed in relationship to others seeking a similar vision.

## Unity: When Life Standing and Falling in the Mosh Pit Is More Than Life on the Stage

The illumination stage for the mystic takes her into the strangest place of all: binding her life to the lives of others and seeking to live not as an individual but as part of something that only makes sense when it is shared. For the Christian mystic this final stage is stage of unity or *unitio*, a period when the soul of the monk and the Spirit of God are bonded together in a union often described in terms of the marriage of the Song of Solomon (also called the Song of Songs, or the Canticle of Canticles) because it is so intimate and core to what is this new life forged after purgation and emptying and into the new light of illumination. For the sonic mystic this journey begins with a movement where the frequency of the soul resonates not only with the art that is drawing him or her higher and deeper, but also with the community of others who share this journey and into the lives of others who the sonic mystic is called to. This unity with other people and the moment of music itself is most perfectly realized in the live performance. This is a moment of ecstatic union marked by ineffable joy, exaltation, and proclamation where we step outside of the small world of our headphones, the safety and isolation of our car, the cocoon of our private homes, and go out into the public space of the club, the stadium, or the open air festival and meet the songs as they come alive not only from the artist but in and through other fans who share the event. This movement into union is at once a proclamation and yet it is also ineffable and moves us beyond language itself. One of the most famous ineffable screams in the U2 canon (cataloging these is a project we will leave to another) is found at 3:02 minutes into "With or without You"—immediately following the acknowledgement of lament that "you give yourself away/ and you give / and you give / and you give yourself away" to the point of extinction, comes a wordless ecstatic release into mystical union as one is released from being outside of sound and becomes one with the sound itself. This is often fleeting in our lives, especially for the sonic mystic who finds these fleeting moments in the midst of a song that lasts only a few minutes. But in the community of fans this moment continues on and on like a divine echo channeled down through the canyons of culture. This is the strange experience I continue to have at live shows as I am pushed by other fans in the pulse of the music. We are at first unsure of each other, almost jealous about this music that is so close to us and unsure that anyone else "gets" it like we do. Then slowly as the show progresses, we forget ourselves and the music brings us together; what was merely a collection of strangers becomes a sea of tuning forks resonating with the vibe, no longer caring who sees us singing along with these lyrics, unafraid that someone will think us juvenile and actually freefalling into the moment-by-moment movement of the show. In rock shows you will see stage diving and people surfing to and fro over your head. In smaller venues with singer-songwriters you will see people tapping their feet and eyes fixed on a point beyond the artist and the stage to another time, another place. As people leave the live show, there is always a solemnness, an active yet quiet rush as the crowd hurries to beat traffic and get home before the evening turns to daylight. Yet this solemnness after a live show has always hit me with a sense of remorse and sadness. Some will write off the live concert experience as escapism. Yet I have found the opposite. It is as if going back to our lives is akin to entering the falsehood and fantasy and leaving the stadium, the club, and open air festival is akin to being cast out of heaven and banished to live east of Eden for the remainder of our days. Yet here is where the sonic mystic differs from many Christians in the new millennium in marked ways. As I watch people leave many churches after a Sunday service, there is almost a sense of relief and a readiness to get on with life, a sense that we have paid our dues to God, sat through the worship service, and can now get back to the business of living our lives for ourselves. It is this difference between what many Christians today consider to be what "the rest of our lives" look like and what our neighbors—the sonic mystics—understand as the role of the mystery, imagination, and transcendence of life that is only glimpsed at in a pop song yet hungered and longed for long after the last encore is played that I hope to recover and dialogue with you about in the pages and songs that fill the rest of this book. There is something lacking in many evangelical Christians lives today—an energy, a playfulness, a willingness to weep when it is time to weep and laugh when it is time to laugh—that is still alive and well in the hearts, minds, and songs of the sonic mystics. It is their music that we need to listen to and their passion and commitment that needs to be taken seriously. For what is the worth of salvation if the life that is lived is so dead and our eyes so vacant that the so-called Good

News that is seen as people drive by a church parking lot on a Sunday morning seems to be "Thank goodness that is over"?

## OPERATING INSTRUCTIONS—SOME THOUGHTS ON USING THIS BOOK

One of the questions I would get while writing this book was, "Why choose *that* song over *this* song?" The question can be asked about the song currently playing on your radio or streaming through your iPod as well. As an avid listener to alternative radio stations both online and over the airwaves, I too am struck with the seemingly random way set lists come together—at times with no rhyme or reason and at other times with the providential punch that has me pulling my car to the side of the road just to fall headlong into the song filling the space and closing out the world rushing by. In some cases the songs I reflect on I chose simply because they speak out in regard to a particular theme core to the Christian faith. Some of the artists are well known; others will seem obscure. But the variety will hopefully demonstrate a unity of sorts that is a key feature of this book— that there is more that holds together the various genres of popular music on our FM dial and MP3 player than separates them. The Beatles hit the nail on the head when they sang "All You Need Is Love"—and every song in this book acknowledges that love in its various faces is what is on everyone's mind—whether it's in a sweet folk ballad, a hip-hop celebration, or a crunchy grunge barnburner. The Christian story is about pushing through the limits of the love we experience only in our subjective understanding and being found by a Love that is beyond all that we can hope for or even imagine. The ache, the longing, the despair, the ecstasy of the songs featured in this book are like puzzle pieces cut out over time and placed together, bit by bit, to form a mosaic that reflects the face of Christ.

*Your Neighbor's Hymnal* can be approached in a number of ways. As an introduction to this stream of popular culture, the overviews and short introductions surrounding each song provide a glossary useful in courses needing texts in theology and popular culture. For use with church groups, be they adult Bible studies or youth groups, the book provides points of reference for connecting key aspects of the Christian faith with illustrations readily available for discussion. For the interested music listener, *Your Neighbor's Hymnal* will provide a means of giving voice to your own musings on faith. Maybe this will be as simple as getting reacquainted with some of the songs that formed you in the past or are now forming the lives of those around you. For some, there may be artists you haven't listened to in years, some you haven't heard of, and some you wish you could forget. Feel free to use the book as a devotional tool of sorts for listening deeper to your music, or simply sit and listen to the songs and reflect upon them with a friend who also loves music.

## Faith, Hope, Love

The book is organized into three sections based around the three grand Christian virtues articulated by Paul in 1 Corinthians 13: faith, hope, and love. Each section includes a number of representative reflections on the history and artist who created the song, some reflections on its lyrical content, and then some theological and biblical connections that will hopefully show some ways in which the song illustrates how your neighbor is hearing, seeking, and finding faith, hope, and love through popular music. Feel free to use these reflections to open up conversations with people you normally don't talk with about the Christian story. In the writing of this book I have had people gather around the songs discussed—akin to a group surrounding a campfire—singing along, kicking their heels to the rhythm, and sometimes clapping their hands over their ears to block out the noise. Music brings people together when words alone cannot—and that is the hope for this book. So sit back, scroll through these selections, find the songs you are familiar with and those that you are not. As mentioned earlier, sometimes it is the music we know from long ago and sometimes it is that new song sung in ways never dreamed of—and sometimes it is the combination of both in a mix tape—that breaks open an opportunity to be released from the old and thrust into the new or even the renewed life illuminated for unity and hope. One last thing: pop music is to be played for joy, so don't work too hard with these songs. Let them wash over you and take a risk as to what you will find on the other side.

# 2
# Faith

FAITH IS A TRICKY term to define and even harder to live out. For some, to have faith is to adhere to certain doctrinal affirmations and creeds. For others, faith is essentially wishful thinking akin to hopefulness where one believes that, as Julian of Norwich mused long ago, "all manner of things shall be well." Others see faith as living into the seemingly improbable or impossible, or an exercise in supreme trust as one leaps into the unknown with complete abandon. The Danish philosopher Søren Kierkegaard is credited with having framed the notion of the "leap of faith" whereby faith is not merely just an intellectual ascent, but a visceral all-or-nothing commitment of body, mind, and soul. Is faith ultimately something we have in ourselves? In other people? In God?

Listening to pop music is in itself an act of faith akin to Kierkegaard's notion of the "leap of faith." For some this leap is provoked by a strong push or awakening that something needs to change, often in the form of conviction. To be convicted by something as an act of faith is to become in some ways overcome and overwhelmed, thoroughly convinced to the point that you are standing at a crossroads and what you now know is incontestable and life as you know it is changed forever. An example of such a moment would be a near-death experience, falling in love, or even hearing Marvin Gaye or Johnny Cash singing for the first time; one may call it a life-defining event. Theologian James Loder sees such moments as acts of faith, for both the secular and sacred come together in such life-defining events. It is in that these "experiences we want eventually to understand in Christian terms are precisely those that reopen the question of reality because the subject of the experience has been convicted by a spiritual presence far greater than the subject him or herself."[1] While Christians may take faith to mean a particular line to a deeper understanding and relationship with God through the person of Jesus Christ, faith can start in many places outside the church, including a seemingly simple pop song that stirs within us something greater than ourselves.

As privatized and individualistic as some people deride pop music as being, it is a medium that continues to encourage people to have life-convicting moments that will move them to play and eventually live out the music for all to hear, joining strangers together through the song and thereby taking the story public in ways that the closed-off lives of many churchgoers often do not on a day-to-day basis. My friend Rev. Beth Maynard, an Episcopal priest, faculty member at Gordon Conwell Seminary, and the author of *Get Up Off Your Knees: Preaching the U2 Catalog*, recently spoke at a conference on the music of U2. I was attending a session on the role that listening to music together in a live show can play in forging a sense of meaning not only for the musician but for the audience members.[2] Drawing from the Christian tradition of worship, Maynard sees modern music fans and concertgoers enacting a practice deep in the liturgical tradition known as *leitourgia*.

## *LEITOURGIA* AS FAN FAITH

As noted by Maynard, the word *leitourgia* is a Greek term used in early Christian communities to mean a public act that expresses the mission of a people, something done in the open and not behind closed doors. Maynard cites David Fagerberg's study *Theologia Prima* in looking at how the term grew in usage in the early Christian communities and notes that the term becomes more and more associated with "actions expressing [a] city's relations to the world of divine powers on which it acknowledged itself to be dependent."[3] In the early centuries of Christianity, *leitourgia* was a term to denote public rather than private gatherings whose focus and intent was essentially to bring light into darkness and challenge the prevailing social and spiritual assumptions of the time. By "public" it is

1. Loder, *Convictional Moment*, 7.

2. Maynard, "U2 Live," presented at the "U2: The Hype and the Feedback" conference, October 4, 2009. My thanks to Rev. Maynard for sharing her insights from her paper with me and providing resources and valuable insights for this notion of *leitourgia*.

3. Fagerberg, *Theologia Prima*, 11.

meant that everyone is invited to participate and find their voice in this reality. As Fagerberg goes on to say, "the early Christians chose the term *leitourgia* for what they were doing [because] it signaled that they did not think themselves to be doing [a service closed off in meaning from the rest of the world], but they were doing the eschatological work of making Christ's kingdom present . . . [embodying] the presence in this world of the Kingdom to come."[4] Faith in this way is that which is so real, so pervasive that it has to be made public and shared, drawing others into the song, challenging the heartbreak and nihilism of an age, and offering an alternative reality for all to see and hear.

In many ways this ancient notion of *leitourgia* is the faith of the pop music fanboy as well. This desire to take something so core to who we are and continue to seek expression for it regardless of what others may think of us is seen in the moment someone becomes so taken with a song and an artist that they play it on repeat for days on end, wear the concert T-shirt, follow the band's Twitter feed and Facebook updates, and have to tell people about it as a way of keeping the world on alert. This is when people forgo the norms set by the culture around them, throw care to the wind, and run fully into expressing something bigger than themselves. A classic example of this is seen in the movement from day-to-day life to attending a rock concert. I recently attended a U2 show with a number of academics. Many of these people were accomplished professors who had written in areas of literary theory, economics, history, sociology, and theology. However, once we stepped into the arena for the rock show and the boys from Dublin took the stage, what had been reserved and mediated discourse became a full-bodied fan fest—PhDs jumping up and down, pumping their fists in the air, dancing in the aisles, and singing along with the thousands of fans gathered under the full harvest moon of November. Amidst the music and flashing stadium lights, people forgot themselves in all the right ways and joined together in chorus after chorus after chorus. Basically, people found faith in something other than themselves and gave themselves over to it even if it was only for a moment.

Alexander Schmemann, writing from the Russian Orthodox tradition, states that for the early Christian community *leitourgia* was a public expression that was the end "of the 'sacred' religious act isolated from and opposed to the 'profane' life of the community."[5] No longer do we keep

4. Ibid., 83.

5. Schmemann, *For the Life of the World.* 26.

what we are passionate about separated from how we organize and live out our lives in the public sphere. To have fanboy faith in the spirit of *leitourgia* is to "out" yourself as a fan and by doing so you allow your faith framed by the music to shape how and why you live in the world. Your priorities change, the people you gather with and for change, and this is not kept locked up but expressed through one's life for the entire world to see. As Schmemann makes clear in reference to the very public expressions of faith in the public sphere for the early Christians, "the pseudo-Christian opposition of the 'spiritual' and the 'material,' the 'sacred' and the 'profane,' the 'religious' and the 'secular,'" is denounced, abolished, and revealed as a monstrous lie about God and man and the world."[6]

It doesn't take a rock show to see this full-bodied faith take hold with a pop song. Just look at the car next to you at the stop light when you hear the thumping of the subwoofer pounding your windows—heads bobbing to the beat like a scene from *Wayne's World*, lip-syncing along to the song and belting it out with all the passion of an *American Idol* finalist. Watch the commuters on the train with their white iPod earbuds. Their eyes are closed, but they're fully alive in ways they won't be during their workday. True, there is pop music fandom that draws people into the trivial and mundane just as there are some Christian worship services that celebrate consumer culture more than critique it or provide an alternative. But the drive to find something larger than ourselves and make it public is a starting point—even a shallow faith is better than no faith at all. And in this we are to celebrate rather than too quickly denounce the fanboy faith that permeates the culture around us. Our neighbor's hymnal is filled with pop songs that are sowing the seeds of faith and pushing for a form of life that is larger than the mundane and points to a transcendence worth paying attention to. People continue to come to pop music as a demonstration of faith in something more than what we often see and do in the so-called real world. It is this rich faith that we will look at in the songs and artists of this section.

## Joni Mitchell—"God Must Be a Boogie Man"

I was at Starbucks a few months back and heard this old track by Joni Mitchell from the 1979 Charlie Mingus tribute album *Mingus*. The story goes that jazz artist Charlie Mingus fell in love with Joni Mitchell's album

6. Ibid., 76.

*Don Juan's Reckless Daughter* and asked if Mitchell would help with a jazz project based upon T. S. Eliot's *Four Quartets*. While the project never got off the ground, Mitchell and Mingus worked together and finished six songs based around themes from T. S. Eliot's masterpiece. The song "God Must Be a Boogie Man" came out of these sessions where a strange artistic trinity of folk singer-songwriter (Mitchell), jazz bassist and certified genius minimalist (Mingus), and one of the greatest poets of the twentieth century (Eliot) fused forms with perpetual fluidity like the dance of the divine Trinity. Such a fusing into a mosaic of artistic flow is in concert with W. B. Yeats's reflections in his poem "Among School Children":

> Labour is blossoming or dancing where
> The body is not bruised to pleasure soul.
> Nor beauty born out of its own despair,
> Nor blear-eyed wisdom out of midnight oil.
> O chestnut-tree, great-rooted blossomer,
> Are you the leaf, the blossom or the bole?
> O body swayed to music, O brightening glance,
> *How can we know the Dancer from the dance?*

Granted the wacky chorus refrain "God must be a boogie man," following Mitchell's calm voice, is a weird reminder that this was composed in the 1970s and they were probably drawing on themes from Andrew Lloyd Webber's *Jesus Christ Superstar* ("He's *dangerous* . . . !") but it's no more difficult to comprehend than the Christian concept of the Trinity *per se*. As Joni Mitchell sings

> He is three
> one's in the middle unmoved
> waiting to show what he sees to the other two
> to the one attacking so afraid
> and the one who keeps trying to love and trust and getting himself
> betrayed
> in the plan . . . the divine plan
> God must be a boogey man.

To listen to Joni Mitchell sing in tension with Mingus's musical signature is to feel the tension of the Trinity in our very lives. Part of faith is learning to live within the tension of being known by a God whose mysterious qualities far outstrip our ability to understand them. Rather than choosing simple certainly or ignorance, we are invited to "sit in" with God's session as children amidst the great dance of the Father, Son, and

Holy Spirit. Like artists coming from very different genres, we too are invited to "make music" in and with the Trinity's work in the world—not to dominate and lead, but to go with the holy flow. This tension is what listening to "God Must Be a Boogie Man" alludes to—artists struggling to find music as a chorus that provides the context for deep questions and uncertainty. It is here that faith begins.

## Blue Scholars—"Burnt Offering"

Hans Christen Anderson published *The Emperor's New Clothes* in 1837 as a commentary regarding the lack of critical assessment in relation to the rise of the new aristocracy in Denmark of the nineteenth century who essentially believed that no one was able to critique them due to their position, wealth, and relative power in society. The story has been told and retold over the past century but is essentially a tale of two weavers of low estate and cultural standing who promise an emperor a new suit of clothes that are invisible to those who are unfit for their position, stupid, or incompetent. When the emperor parades before his subjects in his new clothes, a child cries out, "But he isn't wearing anything at all!" The point of this morality tale is that people become so enamored with the rich and powerful that no one will ever question their actions and they do the most ludicrous things without ever being confronted let alone challenged to change their ways. We live in a time when flashing images of pop stars drive understanding and the written word continues to take a back seat in cultural formation, what we see frames what we believe about God for many people. One of the biggest areas that often goes unchallenged or even commented on from the pulpit is race. Pictures and images of Jesus continue to be white, painting a picture of the Almighty that has become hard to relate to the Scriptures we read let alone the two-millennia witness of the church itself. One famous portrayal in this regard is the famous "Head of Christ" portrait produced by Warner Sallman. Sallman, who died in 1968, was a religious painter and illustrator whose most famous painting is "Head of Christ," which was reproduced more than 500 million times, appearing on church bulletins, calendars, posters, bookmarks, prayer cards, tracts, buttons, stickers, and stationery. As noted in his New York Times article arguing for Sallman to be named the artist of the twentieth century due to his cultural impact, which in many ways eclipses Andy Warhol and Pablo Picasso, William Grimes notes that "tens of thousands of wallet-size copies [of "Head of Christ"] were distributed to servicemen during World War II. In the mid-1950s, Sallman's soulful, back-lighted Jesus with flowing, shoulder-length hair gazed out from the Inspira-Clock and the Inspira-Lamp, tie-in products intended for the pious Protestant home."[7] For generations, Sallman's paintings would hang in homes and churches across the country, offering a mass-produced homogenized Christ that for all intents and purposes was a Swede from Oslo rather than a carpenter's son from Nazareth. For Caucasian youth, there was certainly something to identify with this image—surely this Jesus was "one of us" and offered a resonance to white identity. But what if you were not white? One thing worth noting is that Jesus has been depicted in art through the centuries as a representative of just about every ethnicity on the planet, and this is actually a wonderful, gracious thing. As a multiracial, multicultural Messiah whose bloodstream contains people from all the strata of humanity, seeing the diversity in Christ is vital to understanding who Christ is for the sake of the whole world. Reading Christ's genealogy as outlined in the Gospels of Matthew and Luke is a good place to start. It includes people like Tamar, who is mentioned in Genesis 38 as dressing like a prostitute and seducing Judah in order to provide an heir—an heir, by the way, named Perez, of whom Jesus is a direct descendent. Another member of the family tree is Rahab, who in Joshua 2 is also described as a prostitute who runs a brothel, hid spies sent by Joshua and saved her family as Israel took the city. The red cord she tied to her window signaling that her family was to be protected is said to be the precursor to the phrase "red light district." There is also Ruth, who was descended from the Moabites, who were considered an unclean people (Genesis 19:37). Yet Ruth married Boaz and had a son named Obed (who by Levirate customs is also considered a son or heir to Elimelech, and thus Naomi). In the genealogy which concludes the story, it is pointed out that Obed is the descendant of Perez the son of Judah, and the grandfather of King David and therefore a relation to Jesus. Yet during one of the darkest times in the history of Israel, God chooses someone like Ruth to be a light and give guidance to the people. To get our attention through the years, the coming of Jesus is a portrait of a God who has not chosen to use only lofty platitudes or lofty people to communicate who he is and what he is about. God has time and time again chosen to use the lowly and lofty, the majority and the marginalized, whether walking in purity or laden with the dirt, ash, and twigs of real life, those who don't have all the

7. Grimes, "The Man Who Rendered Jesus."

answers, who doubt from time to time, who get discouraged and bleed when wounded. That is to say, when God has something say or, in the case of this book, sing, it gets wrapped in real people as well as real rhyme.

How would such an image of Christ challenge how we see who and what the incarnation is about? This is the subject of the song "Burnt Offering" by the hip-hop artists Blues Scholars. Their self-titled release was voted "Best Album of 2004" by the Seattle Weekly magazine and is considered one of the key releases that jump-started the hip-hop revival in the Pacific Northwest. Blues Scholars is made up of MC Geologic and DJ/ producer Sabzi, who, as with many hip-hop acts, come from vastly different musical approaches to experiment with the hope of finding a new way to refresh and reimagine not only music but the way people live. Hip-hop as a movement is certainly more than music—it is a holistic approach to life that is committed to authenticity in art, solidarity with all people, and a commitment to equity as generous acts of hospitality. Some will dismiss hip-hop due to its gangsta association with artists who promote violence, misogyny, and bling culture. Yet many hip-hop artists are setting the tone for another way of being. Blues Scholars harken back to artists like A Tribe Called Quest in trying to find a unique, new sound that still echoes the classic boom-bap while reaching forward with social commentary. MC Geo had a start as a battle emcee and spoken-word poet prior to joining up with Sabzi, who trained as a classical and jazz pianist. One of the things that is very evident in their music is how danceable social commentary can be and how spiritual our lives are. Blues Scholars offer poetic lyricism with beats you can dance to that seamlessly blends Marxist commentary with Baha'i spirituality, a monotheistic religion founded in nineteenth-century Persia, emphasizing the spiritual unity of all humankind. This blending of social commentary with spirituality is a tradition seen in many of the artists included in this volume, but how Blue Scholars riffs on influences ranging from Thelonius Monk and Aphex Twin to Marvin Gaye and J Dilla is truly special. In their song "Burnt Offering," the Lord's Prayer is reframed as the artists move deeper into the music and the tension they feel in trying to make sense of faith:

> Our Father
> My art is Heaven, hallowed be
> The drums beating me and my tongue into submission
> I can hardly speak breathing this indelible high
> From an endless supply of Godspeed, and I need

A brand new prayer to read
Seems the old ones grew tons of mold cuz they're narrow as hell
Sometimes they be thinking that this heavens for sale
Worse than that, they still think God is a male
But
Moms used to hang up pictures of white Jesus
Fist clutching rosary beads, over the years
I began to question this Father Almighty
Made in His image but don't look nothing like me
But we be the children of the most high
Ghosts of the colonized lost in the time
Redesign, redefine what it meant to be divine
Knowing that She meant for me to rhyme.

Taking Jesus' prayer for his disciples to emulate and praying it into a new generation, Blue Scholars in many ways fulfill the mandate of the prayer itself. Asking the question of whether the image of Christ that we see hanging on the wall is the Jesus that we really are called to follow, whether we are to blithely mouth a prayer or to enter into it so fully that we ourselves become the prayer by becoming rhyme, challenging the need to have God exclusively male or female and reducing God to only a human level of understanding are all at play in one verse. It is interesting that in "Burnt Offering," they sample soul legend Bill Withers' 1973 track "Kissing My Love," a song that is about the desire for intimacy and closeness. So often music that focuses on a desire for God in the CCM world is a desire of rationality—to have the "mind of Christ" rather than the fullness of the height, breadth, and depth of what a true relationship entails. This is the faith that Blue Scholars are writing about, seeking an image of God that would allow their lives to become the resonant frequency and rhyme of the source of their hope and longings—not merely an unapproachable painting of a bygone era, but an authentic relationship in the here and now.

## Metallica—"Nothing Else Matters"

In my time as a pastor I have performed baptisms, weddings, commissionings, and more funerals than I can count. As one could expect, it is the funerals of those who died too young and those who died tragically that are the most gut-wrenching. Two months after I was ordained, the first funeral I performed was for a young nursing student at the university where I was director of campus ministries. She was a sophomore and, one would think, had the world at her feet—good friends, a vibrant personality, a sharp mind, and a great life ahead of her. Yet one day she drove herself to a nearby park and shot herself. Standing in the midst of students, faculty, and family asking how this could happen is one of the most difficult questions to face when it comes to faith. Another such experience was earlier this year when I officiated a memorial service for a thirty-year-old woman who died of a drug overdose. Her life was difficult in numerous ways but, as testified to by family and friends, she always wanted to become more than her circumstances. She had two children—a sixteen-year-old and a four-year-old. Her parents were divorced and remarried. Her husband speaks very little English. All of this came pouring into the meeting room at the church as we planned for this memorial service. They had been recommended to our church through a series of connections. As we sat and discussed the service, her father pushed a stack of CDs over to me with track numbers. "These are songs that she liked—ones that remind us of her and that she loved to sit and listen to," he said. I looked them over: Sarah McLachlan, Mariah Carey, and . . . Metallica. "Have you heard of them?" he asked. One of the tracks he chose was "Nothing Else Matters" from Metallica's 1991 *Black* album. "These are going to be great," I said, "these will be . . . awesome."

"Nothing Else Matters" is a slow burner to be sure. Written as a Goth ballad, Metallica's lead singer James Hetfield wrote the song with only one hand strumming an E minor chord while he was on the phone with his girlfriend. Since he held the phone with one hand (remember, this is 1991—no Bluetooth earpieces and cell phones were still the size of minivans, but at least down from the monster trucks of the 80s), he plucked the four open strings of a standard E minor chord with the other, which eventually made up the first two bars of the song. It is a song of separation and a deep desire to get closer, written with one hand holding onto the connection to what keeps him alive in this life and using the other to grasp at whatever will turn our longing, our hope, our love into an anthem large enough to fill stadiums. It is a song written so as to not forget what it means to be alive, and to give that gift of life to others through love and faith. The song is about longing for something more and seemed to fit perfectly for this memorial service. As the family and friends came into the fairly standard church sanctuary, more than a couple of eyebrows were raised as the Metallica tune filled the pews and spilled across the floor under the alter and to the foot of the cross that hung on the wall. Tears started to flow as "Nothing Else Matters" became more than a metal ballad but a song of anger, promise, and release wound up in chords and bars and rhythm. The open casket with this young woman's body lay there as the song continued on:

> Never opened myself this way
> Life is ours, we live it our way
> All these words I don't just say
> and nothing else matters
> Trust I seek and I find in you
> Every day for us, something new
> Open mind for a different view
> and nothing else matters
> never cared for what they say
> never cared for games they play
> never cared for what they do
> never cared for what they know
> So close, no matter how far
> Couldn't be much more from the heart
> Forever trusting who we are
> No, nothing else matters.

As the song ran its course, arms covered with more ink than a stack of comic books were rubbing their eyes and waiting for something beyond James Hetfiled's simple tune as we looked toward the cross that hung over that casket. "Nothing Else Matters" opened the way, for "something else" must matter amidst all this sorrow. When people ask me what pop music has to do with theology, it is moments like these I wish I could bottle up and hand to the cynics. People get married, celebrate graduations, drive across the country, and bury their family members to simple pop songs. People continue to seek after something that surrounds and empowers their lives and for this reason I don't believe in the post-Christian jargon some are used to evoking. If there is a post-Christian era I have yet to see that era truly in full bloom. However, the notion of the "after Church" world is certainly true. Granted, the "after church" folks could truly benefit from the deep traditions and meaning found in the ancient church made new in their midst. But when death comes screaming into your world people will act like a proverbial drowning man at sea and will grab the most stable and recognizable thing found floating by. For millions of folks it would not necessarily be the hymnal in church pews but the song on their iPod that reminds them of hope, faith, and love. These crazy songs make sense out of the chaos of life in ways so many other things shoveled at people never do.

As we sat there in the memorial service I had a picture in my mind of this young woman listening to "Nothing Else Matters" and perhaps wishing that as her family and friends gathered they would write one more verse of that song with their very lives—that verse being lives lived remembering her laughter, her love of the sunshine, her passion for music, and what it means to live out this love with others and in the presence of God who lives with us now. As the service continued I read aloud from Psalm 23 and Romans 6:3–9 and spoke of St. Paul's promise that death dies and life will truly live at the end of all things, and I do hope that these words of promise got a grip on folks as they sat there. But I can bet that an old 1991 metal ballad is finding new life for folks and hopefully there is indeed a new verse being written in the lives of this family in deep mourning. That "something else" does matter, that we can reach out not with one hand restrained but embrace each other with both arms fully and experience an even stronger embrace of God's grace and mercy. Some would say that Metallica came to church that day. But I think the gathered were "churched" by James Hetfield and the band in ways we have yet to see the fruit of.

## Vigilantes of Love—"Double Cure"

Bill Mallonee is one of those artists seemingly stuck betwixt and between stardom and obscurity. Bill and his band Vigilantes of Love (VOL) have been critics' darlings since the late 1980s. Bill hails from that alt-country pressure cooker and indie band hive known as Georgia, the same place that spawned such acts as R.E.M., Indigo Girls, the B-52's, and more. Drawing on that singer-songwriter tradition deep in the storytelling psyche of Flannery O'Connor's South, VOL hit the ground running with their first major release on Warner Brothers, *Welcome to Struggleville* (produced by Peter Buck of R.E.M.), and seemed destined to light the world on fire. Then something happened—grunge. With the likes of Screaming Trees, Mudhoney, Soundgarden, Pearl Jam, and Nirvana hitting the sonic sweet spot of the *zeitgeist*, the music marketing guys didn't push VOL and they never seemed to gain the head of steam needed to reach critical mass. VOL has continued to have a loyal following over the years and they have been one of those bands at whose shows you would run into people you would normally hang out with anyway—a following of friends, as it were. I had a chance to spend time with Bill and VOL back in the mid-1990s when they were touring coffeehouses and small venues.

Through some "friends of friends" we had VOL come to the church where I was associate pastor and participate as the worship band for the morning. One of the songs they performed was a new one at the time called "Double Cure." Bill Mallonee referenced one of the key controversies of the Reformation—the notion of *cura animarum*, "cure of souls." Technically, the exercise of a clergy member involves the instruction, by sermons and admonitions, and the sanctification, through the sacraments, of the faithful in a determined district, by a person legitimately appointed for the purpose of *cura animarum*. Those specially ordained for the cure of souls are the Pope for the entire church, the bishops in their dioceses, and the parish priests in their respective parishes. Others may also have part in the cure of souls in subordination to these. For Martin Luther, the responsibility of *cura amimarum* fell upon all believers since the ultimate cure falls upon us all through the work of Christ on the cross. As Bill Mallonee sings in his song, we are called to a "double cure"—the cure of our souls through the saving work of the cross, and in turn, the work of *cura animarum* in the world around us through evangelism and mission. It still amazes me how many sonic mystics get this truth to their core yet so many evangelical Christians do not. Going back to the various big fundraisers for Africa in the 1980s like Band Aid and USA for Africa, through to the (RED) and One.org campaigns, so-called secular pop musicians have been working out this double cure in the world in ways that many Christians are only now catching on to. I have had the chance to consult with a number of churches seeking to find new ways to reach the "unchurched" and the "lost'"—wishing with all the sincerity that they could muster to draw people into their buildings and programs for these lost people's sake. The reality I tell many churches is that what is happening through fans texting support for AIDS orphans at a rock show is more direct to the heart of the "double cure" we are called to than being tangled up in committee meetings. When rock stars are doing aspects of church better than the church . . . it is time the church picked up a new mix tape and started listening to the sonic mystics among us.

VOL was dropped by Warner Brothers and Bill Mallonee continues to plug away as a recording artist. He had a real return to form with his album *Audible Sigh* on Compass Records a few years back, with Emmylou Harris and Gillian Welch backing him up, and he had a great tour through the UK supporting that release. When the band stopped in Glasgow, Scotland, they played a gig at King Tut's Wah Wah Hut—a small music club famous for being the club that launched the careers of Oasis and Franz Ferdinand. We went and saw the show while I was teaching at the University of Glasgow and I had a chance to talk to Bill and the band at the bar after the show. I told him how his music has continued to grow and that the old songs continue to find new meaning with each listen. He smiled and said, "I certainly hope so . . . unless things become new, they stay old." I couldn't agree more.

## Nirvana—"Smells Like Teen Spirit"

Even though the song began as graffiti on the apartment wall by Bikini Kill's Kathleen Hanna after a double date with Dave Grohl, Kurt Cobain, and the "over-bored and self-assured" Tobi Vail, who wore Teen Spirit perfume, Cobain said that "Smells Like Teen Spirit" was ultimately an attack on the apathy of his generation in the 1990s. As Cobain admitted in interviews, the irony is that the great anthem of the grunge movement was musically structured as a 70s pop-rock song—the guitar riffs are taken directly from Boston's "More Than a Feeling." Nevertheless, the tragic genius of Kurt Cobain was the simple fact that he spoke such truth and yet, rather than embracing hope, chose to free-fall into despair. His now infamous suicide note stutters with concern:

> The fact is I can't fool you. Any one of you. It simply isn't fair to you or me. The worst crime I can think of would be to put people off by faking it and pretending as if I'm having 100% fun. Sometimes I feel as if I should have a punch-in time clock before I walk out on stage. I've tried everything within my power to appreciate it, and I do. God, believe me I do but it's not enough.

As the band's name itself attested, Nirvana strove for authenticity in a world of corporate bands that were more concerned with product placement and being the "emo" soundtrack for new Audis. But even for the idealist Cobain, entering the mainstream fray—of big money, huge exposure, massive stadiums filled with would-be disciples in fifty-dollar T-shirts with his picture on them, chanting the lyrics he wrote under a bridge in Aberdeen, Washington, when he was kicked out of his house— inevitably meant an Icarus-like rise and fall. This should not be such a surprise. Waking up each morning and facing both the shadowy reminder of the ideals you professed and the stark reality of what you have become would be dissonance enough for anyone. But as with the myth of Icarus, the higher the flight on waxen wings, the greater the fall.

I am sad that Kurt Cobain's life and death has become so iconic as to verge on cliché; it not only cheapens the tragedy but removes some of the responsibility we as fans have for the life and death of those we venerate through our iPod downloads and T-shirt choices. I am reminded that as Icarus began his naïve ascent toward the sun, his father Daedalus screamed for his return to the earth, that his life made sense with his feet on the ground, that he was created for the earth and not for the air. As Kurt closed his suicide note by paraphrasing Jim Morrison's aphorism à la Neil Young—"it is better to burn out than fade away"—I am reminded how much of the Christian tradition is framed around a similar sentiment: we are in awe of our young martyrs and tragic, embattled heroes and forget about those who "stay the course" and "run the good race." Take the case of Rachel Scott's rise to martyrdom after the 1999 Columbine shootings in America as an example of someone who died at a young age yet led a life of moral integrity and knew the value of loving others more than oneself.

In his great biography of Kurt Cobain entitled *Heavier than Heaven*, Charles Cross discusses how formative the experiences of Kurt Cobain and Krist Novoselic were growing up in rural Aberdeen, and, specifically, their experience in a Baptist youth group. Cobain had a few significant conversion experiences in his youth and spoke passionately about a desire to know God at a deep level. The reality, he said, is that God won't be there for us when we need him most. In many ways, Cobain's career was the ultimate daring of God to intervene, a pushing of the boundaries so hard as to awaken the supposedly sleeping God and know his presence in our times of darkness.

Listening to "Smells Like Teen Spirit" today, more than two decades after its release at the dawn of the grunge movement, makes me realize how influential it continues to be and reminds me how great it really is. One of the timeless refrains that haunts me in the song is "Here we are now, entertain us." It is sung as a dare from the mosh pit of a generation looking up at the stage inhabited by authority figures who have disappointed them over and over again. And yet these same authority figures found ways to keep their children occupied; through television, video streaming, and other forms of entertainment, the hope was that even though their parents were off working for the American dream, the kids would—to riff on the Who—"be alright." Yet here is the song of a generation in the early 1990s, after the Reagan era and poised for the great wealth bubble of the late 90s, chanting that there is no entertainment left that will cause them to fall asleep again. No, this was a grunge generation that was very much awake and ready to do something, anything . . . if there was just something worth doing. In this way, "Smells Like Teen Spirit" is one of the most profound cries for faith that a generation has cried through a pop song. As triumphant and exhilarating as the song is, it is the tension between the music and the lyrics, where the former is revving its engine and the lyrics are running and stumbling just to catch up, that lends notes of tragedy to it. If there is a cover version that really speaks the song anew in the twenty-first century, I recommend Tori Amos's cover on her *Crucify* EP. Amos was one of the first to cover "Smells Like Teen Spirit" yet saw the truth of the song wasn't found in the speed and volume that Nirvana first recorded it, but in the stillness and quiet of the verses set to a plaintive piano. As much as "Smells Like Teen Spirit" was a bombastic cry to awaken the "over-bored and self-assured" of our generation, it is fitting to hear it as the dirge and funeral march of ideals that Kurt Cobain was never able to live into.

### Johnny Cash—*My Mother's Hymn Book*

I came to Johnny Cash via the eight-track player in my family's 1972 VW Bus. The eight-track is something of a time stamp these days. Those who remember clicking that big brick of tape into the player have a carbon dating akin to "So, where were you when Kennedy was shot?" Our VW had a random assortment of eight-tracks that would be cycled through on family road trips—the Statler Brothers, John Denver, Cat Stevens, Barry Manilow, and the Man in Black, Johnny Cash.

Frankly, I was introduced to the "wrong" Cash—bad currency, if you will. I listened to the hokier era of Cash's career while reading Daredevil comics in the back of the VW Bus—such tunes as "A Boy Named Sue" and "Look at Them Beans!" But the voice stayed with me, like a canyon dug out over centuries only waiting for a flood to fill it. The fact remains that Johnny Cash has tallied more pop hit singles than most bestselling musicians to date. Against the likes of Barbara Streisand, Michael Jackson (including his Jackson 5 hits), The Four Seasons, David Bowie, The Supremes, Elton John, Billy Joel, Kenny Rogers, Simon and Garfunkel, Martin Gaye, B. B. King, Roy Orbison, Kool & the Gang, Linda Ronstadt, Diana Ross, the Osmond Family, or Jerry Lee Lewis, Johnny Cash reigns supreme as a hit maker. As someone who has shaped not only modern music but American culture as a whole, there are few people who can touch the Man in Black.

It is the end of Cash's career that remains with me thanks to the phoenix-like rise from the flames he has had in the past decade with Rick Rubin and his *American Recordings*. Rubin did a very basic thing: he wanted to look beyond the music and find that voice, a one-of-a-kind original that had such a fragile honesty that it could unlock any song it worked with. Those last albums earned him Grammys: Best Folk Album (1994) for *American Recordings*; Best Country Album (1998) for *Unchained*; and Best Country Male Vocal Performance (2000) for *Solitary Man*. Cash received the most coveted Grammy award, for Lifetime Achievement, in 1999.

One of his last recordings was *My Mother's Hymn Book*, a collection of the hymns included in his amazing box set *Unearthed* and later released as a separate album. These are spirituals he grew up with as a child of the Oklahoma cotton fields. It is just Cash and his guitar as he sings hurt and longing into standard hymns that it is enough to bring you to silence. That voice and that honesty have earned him the right to be heard on alternative stations like KEXP and have caused him to be turned away by so-called Christian radio. In a time when authenticity is looking for a voice, Johnny Cash's voice calls us back to a depth and faith in our listening that few artists offer. Cash reminds us that suffering and loss forged into song can invite listeners to lose themselves in the stillness of hope and light wrestling with darkness. It is on this soil where light and dark wrestle that faith sends its deepest roots, reaching ever deeper into the darker soils for its grounding and sustenance, and bears its fullest fruit in the dawning daylight. This is the faith that is the real thing and worthy of a real life.

## Lee Greenwood—"God Bless the USA"

Faith is a term that people will employ in reference to that which gives them identity. Faith in family, in the economy, or for that matter, in one's country. As I write this, we're coming up on Independence Day weekend in the United States. That means illegal fireworks, barbeques with hot dogs and hamburgers, little children wearing patriotic garb, and the sounds of what many consider to be the most recognizable patriotic song in the nation blaring from coast to coast. If you think I'm talking about the "The Battle Hymn of the Republic" or even Springsteen's "Born in the USA," think again.

As Lee Greenwood points out in his personal bio on his website, his musical career had humble beginnings on a farm outside of Sacramento, California.[8] After years of struggling to gain recognition in the music industry working the lounges of Las Vegas, in 1983 Greenwood got that one hit that would change his life forever: "God Bless the USA." 1983 remains a stellar year in the history of pop culture: *Dallas* and *The A Team* were tops on TV; in music U2's *War* launched the band into America, R.E.M.'s stunning *Murmur* album came out; the Police released their last album, *Synchronicity*, and Run-D.M.C.'s eponymous debut album hit the charts making rap a household name. But it was the gift of Ronald Reagan's revisioning of America that transported Lee Greenwood far beyond the ranks of stardom to a niche in America's pop culture that seems forever reserved for him and him alone. Every movement needs a soundtrack, and Greenwood's "God Bless the USA" fit the bill.

If any doubt existed of Greenwood's enduring imprint on America, it was dispelled in 2003—the twenty-year anniversary of its release—when "God Bless the USA" was voted as the most recognizable patriotic song in the nation. The song that Lee Greenwood wrote bested all the other contestants, including "God Bless America" and "The Star-Spangled Banner," as the modern national anthem of the common man.

"Since the tragedies of September 11," Greenwood's website states,

> Lee has seen his signature hit "God Bless the USA." take on yet another incarnation. Since the attack on America, airplay has increased tenfold, skyrocketing "God Bless the USA" back into the Top 20 of the Billboard country airplay chart, and sending Lee's 1992 album *American Patriot* to the top of the sales charts. The album was certified gold in October 2001 & platinum in December 2001. In January of 2002, Lee signed a long-term recording contract with Curb Records. As 2003 marks the 20th anniversary of the patriot hymn, its emotional impact was proven yet again, as Americans nationwide embraced its message in March 2003 when the United States engaged in Operation Iraqi Freedom.[9]

Needless to say, the song has legs to run and continues to do so twenty-plus years after its release. As an unofficial patriotic anthem, it is certainly one that argues for a joining of church and state in ways to which the Declaration of Independence doesn't seem to allude:

8. Greenwood, "Bio," http://www.leegreenwood.com/index.php?p=360.

9. General Entertainment, "Lee Greenwood."

I'm proud to be an American
where at least I know I'm free,
And I won't forget the men who died
who gave that right to me,
And I gladly stand up next to you
and defend her still today,
'Cause there ain't no doubt
I love this land
God bless the USA.

Granted, Greenwood's lyrics are a prayer for blessing and remembrance rather than an invocation of triumph, but the sense of "favored-nation status" is hard to ignore. Can we sing songs of overt patriotism—especially a song that so expressly invokes God's favor—when nationalism is dispelled under Christ's vision of the kingdom of God in the Sermon on the Mount? Every nation-state has its equivalent of "God Bless the USA" that patriotism rises during times of stress and trial as a way to give confidence, support, and structure when the prevailing movements may leave us without. As people seek hope and guidance from pop songs, they can also turn up the volume so loud and sing the lyrics without reflection to force out the fears and longings that rest just below the surface. As mentioned in this section, faith is something that is part and parcel to pop songs. People turn to them to find something beyond these troubled times, to seek a vision for a life yet to come and a hope yet to be realized. Yet sometimes the songs we choose can also deafen us to what Abraham Lincoln called "the angels of our better nature" and create a vision for what it means to be part of a community or nation. In this we need to remember that the songs we choose will shape us and the way we view others. If we are to sing "God Bless the USA" perhaps it would be helpful to keep in mind some thoughts from Swiss theologian Karl Barth. In 1933 Barth and other leaders challenged the church in Germany to make a stand against nationalism as the defining feature of authentic faith through drafting what is known as the Barmen Declaration. As noted in the Barmen Declaration, National Socialism in Germany in the 1920 and 30s had co-opted the way in which the German church understood what its purpose was, and this was is a deeply theological concern:

> the fact that the theological basis, in which the German Evangelical Church is united, has been continually and systematically thwarted and rendered ineffective by alien principles, on the part of the

leaders and spokesmen of the "German Christians" as well as on the part of the Church administration. When these principles are held to be valid, then, according to all the Confessions in force among us, the Church ceases to be the Church and the German Evangelical Church, as a federation of Confessional Churches, becomes intrinsically impossible.[10]

The danger of patriotism, like any -ism, is the way that it can frame and effectively distract people from that which is truly worth fighting and dying for. I believe that God has blessed a good many people and, along with Lee Greenwood, think that some of that blessing is with the people who make up the USA. But if a song directs me away from the source of blessing and puts my faith in the place where some of that blessing falls, then there is a problem. In this faith and patriotism have always made strange bedfellows, and this is where the writing of new songs is something that we need all the more.

## The Band—"The Weight"

One of the things that makes faith a living thing for people are the choices that we make to completely commit ourselves to a course of action, a way of life, a belief so deep and grounding that everything changes as a result. In one sense this is the patriotic passion we reflected on in the previous section. These moments of decision are often described as standing at a crossroads and taking a step that commits us to one course of action over another. The crossroads are a strange wilderness area in life. Things inhabit, grow, and often thrive at the point of crossroads that don't seem to exist anywhere else. Case in point: every day when I drive Washington State highway 527 from Mill Creek through the city of Bothell and come to the end of the road, I must choose to go right or left. This particular crossroads is the location of the Washington State Ferret Rescue and Shelter. Every morning I take that right-hand turn and my peripheral vision catches the weather-beaten sign hanging half shackled to an abandoned apartment building identifying the locus of ferret advocacy for the Pacific Northwest. Anywhere else this beat-up sign with its bizarre mission statement would seem out of sorts, but not at this place-between-places.

In short: strange things are made normal at crossroads.

10. Barmen Declaration, 8.07. The full document may be found in Cochrane, *Church's Confession under Hitler*, 237–42.

I had a similar experience when I watched Martin Scorsese's 1978 rockumentary *The Last Waltz*. I had been meaning to watch it for quite a while and finally took the dive after seeing a five-dollar DVD version in a bargain bin at Safeway. In so many ways, *The Last Waltz* lives up to the hype—it really is one of the best rock-and-roll films ever. The film chronicles the last concert of the last tour of The Band (Rick Danko, Levon Helm, Garth Hudson, Rickey Manuel, and Robbie Robertson), one of the best late-70s acts to grace the stage. The film begins rather Quentin Tarantino-esque by starting at the end, with an encore of a cover of Marvin Gaye's "(Baby) Don't Do It." From there the movie progresses through some standard rockumentary asides, with members of The Band waxing lyrical about their careers and relationships, and various luminaries from rock history—Eric Clapton, Bob Dylan, Dr. John, Emmylou Harris, and Muddy Waters, to name a few (seeing Neil Diamond sporting shades that are now back in fashion is dead brilliant)—take the stage to send them off to pasture.

What is particularly great about the film is Scorsese's use of 35-millimeter film and multiple camera angles to create a lush, deep feel to the visuals as well as three staged pieces, each of which features a classic song from The Band's catalogue. These set pieces feel like a larger-than-life operetta, obscenely grand in scope and large in feel—imagine a rock video framed with the care of a 1940s MGM production like *Gone with the Wind*. Scorsese shot these scenes on huge soundstages and filled the visuals with soft light gels and eerie dry ice effects so that you are not sure where you are in time and space. Of the three set pieces, the visual and sonic production of The Band's classic "The Weight," is noteworthy. Scorsese invited the Staples Singers to join The Band for the song, an addition that turned out magical. Mavis Staples continues to be one of the great voices in blues and gospel, having sung with Bob Dylan and many others. There is just something distinctly "other" about this pairing of a Southern-flavored bar band and three gospel singers coming together in a song that speaks of putting burdens on and taking burdens off.

Robbie Robertson speaks of writing "The Weight" in this way:

> When I wrote "The Weight," the first song for *Music from Big Pink*, it had a kind of American mythology I was reinventing using my connection to the universal language. The Nazareth in "The Weight" was Nazareth, Pennsylvania. It was a little off-handed— "I pulled into Nazareth." Well I don't know if the Nazareth that

Jesus came from is the kind of place you pull into, but I do know that you pull into Nazareth, Pennsylvania! I'm experimenting with North American mythology. I didn't mean to take sacred, precious things and turn them into humor.[11]

However, listening to "The Weight" backed by the Staples sisters sounds like a strange crossroads convergence of worlds layered. Its American trucker mythos is mixed with New Testament typology—there is "no room at the inn," but this Nazareth is set in both an American landscape and a backwater Middle Eastern village. The guy of the manger past and honky-tonk present is a-skinnin' and a-grinnin' but has zero to offer. The song offers a crossroads and overlapping of worlds with a repeating theme that transcends time and place. It might be that a rock musician pulls into Nazareth, Pennsylvania, but if so, Nazareth warps itself first into the biblical town and then into a Western town before his eyes.

> I pulled into Nazareth
> Was feelin' about half past dead
> I just need some place where I can lay my head
> "Hey, Mister can you tell me where a man might find a bed?"
> He just grinned and shook my hand
> And "no" was all he said.

This crossroads of American myth and biblical landscape is certainly a part of rock music and something that people instinctively connect with. Why the church needs to be so overt at making connections to the faith tradition when people's imagination seems hardwired to make these connections remains a mystery to me. If rock musicians understand this, why can't the church?

We all seem to live in the convergence zone of our past, present, and future lives, like in a *Quantum Leap* episode—that great 1980s sci-fi show that had a character leaping in and out of lives in the past trying to correct the wrongs done so that the future might become a better place. The convergence offered by Scorsese shows that living at the crossroads is always more interesting than getting to where you are going. The crossroads of The Band's last hurrah brought a transcendent wrinkle to a familiar tune and carried it to another level.

Whether saving ferrets or getting the load off our brother's back, the crossroads continues to be an interesting place, especially to find and fuel

---

11. Cited in Cocks, "Down to Old Dixie and Back."

faith. Many sonic mystics are standing at this same crossroads and perhaps this is a place for the church to go to as well.

### Steve Earle—"John Walker's Blues"

As discussed previously, faith is often wrapped with patriotism for Americans and emboldened in songs. And yet as seen in The Band's song "The Weight," many pop songs bridge the mythology of where we are with the mythic, keeping that tension in play as we live life at the crossroads—a place that is neither here nor there but always on the way somewhere and often a place we have never dreamed. As people seek to have faith in something, and certainly the pop songs that populate the airwaves and downloads of sonic mystics speak to this fact, how this notion of national identity plays into faith is important. I admit asking myself this question at odd times these days—driving down the freeway past the fourteenth Wal-Mart I've seen in ten miles, watching celebrities on the news after every major disaster running to the disaster area with his or her PR agent in tow to photograph, the simplicity of watching kids in a sandlot play America's great pastime September evening, like a real-life version of a Norman Rockwell painting.

Writing songs and albums that are attempts at capturing what it means to be American is as old as Cole Porter. Whether gushing patriotism or protesting Uncle Sam with righteous indignation, pop music has been a medium to define and ultimately promote a particular slant on the USA. Perhaps the battle to define what it means to be American in the four-minute pop song stems from the fact that no artistic form in recent memory has captured the shape of the American soul—immediately accessible and easy to sing along with even if the melody is forgotten. Some songs, however, can bridge worlds, place us at the crossroads of a world we only think we know and a world yet to come, and force us to reconsider things that perhaps need to be reconsidered. One such artist that many people listen to but who doesn't get airplay on Christian radio is Steve Earle.

If you haven't gotten into Steve Earle, know that he's a national treasure or, depending upon your views, a traitor. For the past two decades, Earle has been one of the more compellingly engaged figures on the American cultural landscape. He is the author of bestselling works of fiction (like *Doghouse Roses*, for example) and a playwright. Best known as an alt-country musician *par excellence*, his contribution to the merging of progressive country with the wider rock audience remains huge. Indeed, there is every reason to believe that the entire genre of alt-country would not exist had it not been for Earle's groundbreaking extension of what used to be called "folk rock." His recorded work, from the classic 1986 *Guitartown* onward through such excitingly heartfelt and redemptive works as *Copperhead Road, I Feel Alright, El Corazon*, and *Transcendental Blues*, to recent albums like *The Revolution Starts . . . Now*, represents an extraordinary catalogue of deeply personal music that compares favorably with such esteemed heroes as Neil Young, Bruce Springsteen, and even Bob Dylan.

In describing *Jerusalem*, Steve Earle's sixth album in under six years, Earle says,

> This is a political record because there seems no other proper re-sponse to the place we're at now. But I'm not trying to get myself deported or something. In a big way this is the most pro-American record I've ever made. In fact, I feel *urgently* American. I under-stand why none of those congressmen voted against the Patriot Act, out of respect for the Trade Center victims' families. I've sat in the death house with victims' families, seen them suffer. But this is an incredibly dangerous piece of legislation. Freedoms, American freedoms, things voted into law as American freedoms, everything that came out of the 1960s, are disappearing, and as any patriot can see, that has to be opposed.[12]

One of the most controversial songs of any artist in recent memory is the song "John Walker's Blues," which deals with John Walker Lindh, the Marin County teenager and admitted Taliban fighter. The song opens with the lines, "Just an American boy, raised on MTV. . . . I seen all the boys in the soda pop bands and none of them looked like me." and finishes with a recitation of Sura 47, verse 19 of the Qur'an. Earle wrote the song as the newspapers were clamoring for Walker to be strung up for treason.

> Would I be upset if [my son] suddenly turned up fighting for the Islamic Jihad? Sure, absolutely. Fundamentalism, as practiced by the Taliban, is the enemy of real thought, and religion too. But there are circumstances. Walker was from a very bohemian household, from Marin County. His father had just come out of the closet.

---

12. Steve Earle, cited by David Hill, "Review of *Jerusalem*," in *Denver Westword Music* (Nov 21, 2002). Online: http://www.westword.com/2002-11-21/music/steve-earle/.

It's hard to say how that played out in Walker's mind. He went to Yemen because that's where they teach the purest kind of Arabic. He didn't just sit on the couch and watch the box, get depressed and complain. He was a smart kid, he graduated from high school early, the culture here didn't impress him, so he went out looking for something to believe in.[13]

The album is tight and the questions it raises are simply electric. Earle says *Jerusalem* is his "most Old Testament record," noting that "I've only got one chick song on it, the one I sing with Emmy [Emmylou Harris]." His critique of fear-based paranoia ("Conspiracy Theory") seems to be more true today than ever.

However, even at its most apocalyptic—with the likes of the opening track, "Ashes to Ashes," which feels at home alongside Tom Waits's "Earth Died Screaming"—*Jerusalem* is essentially an album of hope. As Earle states:

> I am really optimistic. That's the idea of *Jerusalem*, the last cut on the disk you hear the bad news. You know it is not a lie. What happened on 9/11 was a horror, what happens every day in Israel and Palestine can be a horror. But you try to see past that. You have to believe this will be better. To some redemption, I'm someone who has always wanted to believe. I'm good at it.[14]

Maybe being American is something more than America after all. Maybe the idea that formed that drive to find the New Jerusalem across the Atlantic over two hundred years ago still animates and illumines the hearts and minds of artists willing to ask hard questions and sing difficult words in a hope beyond hope. Maybe it points us toward concerns outside our national interests and toward a humility of Kingdom-centric love. As Earle muses in the closing song "Jerusalem":

> And there'll be no barricades then
> There'll be no wire or walls
> And we can wash all this blood from our hands
> And all this hatred from our souls
> And I believe that on that day all the children of Abraham
> Will lay down their swords forever in Jerusalem.

13. Steve Earle, cited in David McGee, *Steve Earle: Fearless Heart, Outlaw Poet* (San Francisco: Backbeat, 2005) 254.

14. Steve Earle, introduction to "Jerusalem," online: http://www.steveearle.com.

### The Beatles—"Yesterday"

Songs don't make memories, but certain songs certainly bookmark them for us and eventually stain those memories with their rhythm and lyrical flow. To be human is to have memories that are often forged to our deepest longings—our childhood wonder of catching a snowflake on our tongue for the first time, the angst-ridden shame of wanting to fit into a conversation at school and being tuned out, the awe of falling in love and the humility of the small things that keep love alive. Along the way music provides both a canvas upon which our memories gain their shape and hue and an earthy bed into which memories develop deep and abiding roots. We nurture our glad memories' growth by tending this garden of the past—pruning and shaping the good and killing off the bad. Yet our ability to tend the garden of our past only goes so far when an unannounced pop song comes on the radio in a crowded party or fills the sonic space of a coffee shop. In an instant we are thirteen years old, or twenty-two, or thirty-five, or forty-one, all over again. Memories long dormant are clicked open like a hyperlink to the soul. Memories awaken and with them the all-too-real emotions flood us in a torrent.

I think this is the irony of the Beatles' classic, "Yesterday." The memories continue to circle the central character like a hawk, pulling him back to his past, which is his true present:

> Yesterday,
> All my troubles seemed so far away,
> Now it looks as though they're here to stay,
> Oh, I believe in yesterday.
>
> Suddenly,
> I'm not half the man I used to be,
> There's a shadow hanging over me,
> Oh, yesterday came suddenly.

This ironic turn—the present is only found in the past ("yesterday came suddenly")—is a core facet of the Christian faith and certainly true in how and why people gravitate to pop songs over and over again. We recognize the sounds of our past and they become recovered, reanimated, and then grafted into us anew to bear fruit that is sourced equally from the roots we have established in the present and the branches brought back to life from our yesterdays. The trends in pop music speak to this so well. Rockabilly reaches back to country, hip-hop reaches back to Delta blues, pop ballads reach back to the folk traditions of generations of immigrants lamenting the loss of love and the hope for reunion. This bringing together of the past and the present in order to ready oneself for what the future holds is present in the Christian sacraments as well. Like pop songs, the sacraments are played over and over again with each generation acting as a cover band taking up the well-worn tune with new instruments yet a tradition to rest upon. The Eucharist itself teaches us how present the past truly is. We remember our present even more than we live it, or we live our past best by remembering it anew. The fact that the Eucharist is the Lord's Supper only in the *act* of remembering should remind us that memory is essential to what makes faith real.

Or maybe just listening to the Beatles from time to time is a good thing.

## Shirley Caesar—"Gotta Serve Somebody" by Bob Dylan

As I mentioned in the earlier reflection, people of faith are essentially a cover band—taking the songs that have served the generations before it and making them their own by singing them with passion into the time and place in which they live and breathe. One of the ways that some CCM artists have sought to find crossover appeal outside of the CCM market is to take on so-called secular songs and cover them, thereby keeping a hand "in the world" but, by changing the words or arrangement, not being "of the world." Since CCM took the music industry by storm back in the late 1970s and early 80s, some artists have crossed over from the CCM world (Amy Grant, Sam Phillips), but the singing of cover songs hasn't really convinced many sonic mystics and the reason isn't a matter solely of lack of skill. In order to truly cover a song you need, akin to the prophets of old, to devour it and make it a part of you.

I remember watching Martin Scorsese's rockumentary on Bob Dylan, entitled *No Direction Home*. The PBS film was incredibility focused, a very human look at the singer-songwriter's life and music from 1961 to 1966. It chronicled the years when Bob Dylan moved from being merely another folk singer to being a true American icon. What I was most taken by were the raw, vulnerable interviews of Dylan in 2005 as he reflected on his life and art. More than once he mused that "Hibbing [his home-town] was nowhere—I came from nowhere—my family didn't influence me. I left Hibbing and made myself."[15] There was a stark amorality to his reflections. Beholden to no one, meaning was something found only in the "now." Most telling in this regard were the interviews with those who were closest to him during these years. Listening to Joan Baez, it was as if Dylan honestly didn't realize that the world around him was in turmoil. As she put it, people think that his songs denoted a level of commitment to certain political views—taking a stand against Vietnam, opposing racial injustice, and so forth. What made his songs powerful, she said (as did Mavis Staples), was the transcendent quality of life that he sang about. That power was manifest when his songs, along with the growing mythos of Bob Dylan, were taken on by other artists. Even though "the artist known as Bob" never did sit-ins in protest, his spirit was breathed into the millions that sang his songs amidst *their* actions of protest, and it gave the songs flesh. The songs became, along with Dylan himself, protest songs.

In a similar way, the Columbia Records compilation from a few years back, entitled *Gotta Serve Somebody: The Gospel Songs of Bob Dylan*, takes the flesh of Dylan's more faith-centric tunes and gives them Holy Spirit power through the voices of true gospel artists. Dylan's dance with Christianity—including the famed harmonica backing for early Christian rocker Keith Green—is the stuff of legend. The late John Bauldie heard from Tony Wright, the artist who Dylan hired to paint the original cover to the *Saved* album, that

> when he was doing the previous album, *Slow Train Coming*, in Muscle Shoals, he'd had this vision of Jesus, of the hand coming down and these hands reaching up. And he said at the same time he had this vision, he saw the whole album too—all the songs, everything, the whole thing was there. And he said, "What you've drawn here was exactly what I saw."[16]

In a similar vein, the gospel artists on *Gotta Serve Somebody* sing what they see as the event horizon of Dylan's songs, many of which are often dismissed by Dylan fans from his *Saved* and *Shot of Love* era but deserve the proper context to be heard.

The first track has gospel great Shirley Caesar starting off with a call-to-worship pre-song rap that includes these words: "I wanna share Bob Dylan's song with you." As one reviewer noted:

15. Shelton, *No Direction Home*, 16.
16. Marshall, *Restless Pilgrim*, 123.

It may well be the case that she's done to "Gotta Serve Somebody" what Jimi Hendrix did to "All Along the Watchtower." Like Hendrix, she wasted no time in making it her own and devoured it. Dylan even said, way back in 1985, that he liked her version better than his. Caesar's performance, which makes heartfelt and emotional declarations that seem anything but weak, alludes to the Hebrew Scriptures at the beginning of the song (Joshua) and at the end (Chronicles). So do her backup singers, with their occasional "serve my Jesus."[17]

The lost boy from Hibbing, Minnesota, has certainly written some great tunes, many of which, it seems, speak of a home in ways his "never-ending tour" only begins to touch on.

If you get a chance, pick up a copy of *Gotta Serve Somebody*—even if you can't stand Bob Dylan's voice. These artists will get you out of your seat and dancing in the aisle. And it speaks to the act of faith that in order to understand a song, like Shirley Ceasar, you can't do it halfway and expect anyone to be listening when you are done. If the church was a cover band for its tradition with as much abandon as Shirley Ceasar, I guarantee the sonic mystics would be paying attention.

## The Jackson 5—"ABC" (from *Motown Remixed*)

My freshman university students that I teach were *born* in the 1990s. Just let that sink in for a second. This is a generation for whom "cut and paste" has never entailed picking up a pair of scissors. A 2005 issue of *Wired* magazine recently trumpeted the "cut and paste" cultural revolution with the likes of cyberpunk godfather William Gibson's statement that modern cultural history from the beat poets through to the the JarJar-less "Phantom Edit" is nothing novel, but a mash-up of influences remixed for easy consumption and instant access.

One such celebration of remixing that is on my iPod is *Motown Remixed*, which is the respinning and mashing up of Motown artists by DJs, hip-hop and trip-hop artists. As mentioned in the previous reflection, the art of the cover song is truly a sacramental engagement that requires a merging of the past with the present without holding back—a complete abandon and release akin to the purgation of mystics and the release into illumination so many sonic mystics desire. Does the cover artist attempt

17. Scott Marshall and Marcia Ford, *Restless Pilgrim: The Spiritual Journey of Bob Dylan* (Lake Mary, FL: Relevant, 2004) 130.

to honor the original artist by merely mimicking every aspect of the song as it was first recorded, or is it a form of honoring the original artist to take the direction set by the song and add a new signature? Much of this comes to how we understand the sacraments in themselves, I suppose.

Take the remixed version of The Jackson 5's classic "ABC." When Salaam Remi remixed the song, he didn't crush the song under the weight of additional techno funk. Rather, to discover the song, he opened it up, isolating all the individual tracks and systematically relaying them with time delays of microseconds to give "space." The bass and drum loops give room and don't crowd. What I heard anew in this remix was the amazing innocence in Michael Jackson's voice. But what is also telling is the minor key Indian bhangra-enhanced chimes that give the all-too-knowing sound that this young boy is doomed to live in a minor key. Indeed, given what has happened, it is at times painful and at times illuminating to let this young voice be young once again. In an age of sampling and mash ups, it is tempting to dismiss artists like Kanye West and Jay Z as merely feeding off someone else's art. Yet, like a mosaic painfully rendered from broken shards cast off in the dust and made into a beautiful whole that is at once complete yet fractured, what DJs and hip-hop artists can do is recover and redeem something, remove a generation of preconceived notions regarding a song, and shock us into something akin to Paul's journey on the Damascus road or the moment when Bob Dylan went electric. Sometimes we need to remix the past to truly appreciate how far we have come, or how far we have fallen.

## Neil Diamond—"Brother Love's Traveling Salvation Show"

There is a certain cycle to life, a movement that can begin with crisis, result in deep-seated shame and anger, and then move through healing, reconciliation, and yes, peace and contentment. This pretty much sums up my relationship with Neil Diamond.

Let me go back to the 1970s, those golden halcyon days of youth where I was beginning to understand that being ten years old included establishing myself as "cool." This entailed a certain level of image management: grape ripple Goodie comb sticking out of the back of the Sears Toughskins, pooka shells around the neck—you get the picture. My cooler-than-cool friends introduced me to the wonder of disco and all those "conjunction" bands like Kool and the Gang, KC and the Sunshine Band, and Earth, Wind & Fire. However, stepping into the family VW

Campervan was a story in geek fear writ large. Of the four or five eight-track tapes we owned, the majority of playtime was devoted to the Jazz Singer himself, Neil Diamond. I just tuned him out as much as I could and hoped that my folks didn't put any music on when it was our turn to drive my friends home. Friends of mine would talk about their parents going to cool concerts, but the only concerts I remember my folks ever attending were Neil Diamond shows. In a sense, it was almost liturgical. Neil Diamond would bring his big floor show to Seattle every fall and sell out the Seattle Center Arena for a week stay. It was my annual pre-Advent nightmare. The LP albums would plop onto the turntable and Neil would start singing about "butterscotch sticking to all his senses." To a ten-year-old, it just sounded, well, gross.

Fast forward a few decades . . .

I don't know if it is a sonic narcotic or what, but now I see the light: Neil Diamond is the original emo boy. Before Bright Eyes, before Elliott Smith, before Death Cab, before Arcade Fire, before Iron and Wine, there was "I Am I Said . . . to no one there . . ." He also was very interested in the performative nature of religion—that faith is only faith when it is emotive and vibrant as well as thoughtful. One of the songs I consider a guilty pleasure is "Brother Love's Traveling Salvation Show," a great tribute to the tent revival preaching of the Southland. The song builds from the lyric that would become the title of his platinum-selling live album (with one of the most suggestive album covers to boot), *Hot August Night*:

> Hot August night
> And the leaves hanging down
> And the grass on the ground smelling sweet
> Move up the road
> To the outside of town
> And the sound of that good gospel beat.

As the gospel choir preps the song, building in volume, Diamond struts in. No longer is he Yussel Rabinowitz, a talented cantor from *The Jazz Singer*, but a revivalist preacher ready to "turn and burn" a room:

> Room gets suddenly still
> And when you'd almost bet
> You could hear yourself sweat,
> he walks in
> Eyes black as coal
> And when he lifts his face

Every ear in the place is on him
Starting soft and slow
Like a small earthquake
And when he lets go
Half the valley shakes.

Whether evoking images from *Night of the Hunter* or *The Apostle*, Diamond does a great job of making a revival into a sing-along. One of the things I love about pop music is that it is an open field and you don't have to be born into it nor come from royalty to get a shot. It is just a great reminder that even though Diamond's career has certainly taken the all-too-painful turn toward self-parody (albeit a *lucrative* self-parody—Diamond's 2005 box office haul was more than $42.4 million from forty-three shows, thirty-six of them sellouts) he still can write a great song.

However, this parody changed that year when in 2005 Rick Rubin, the wunderkind producer noted for restoring Johnny Cash's glory through the *American Recordings* series, produced a spare, raw album by Diamond entitled simply *12 Songs*, which turned out to be an artistic shocker—not only could Neil Diamond glam it up, he could still write great songs and perform them. Inducted into the Rock and Roll Hall of Fame in 2011, the genius that is Neil Diamond is finally and for all time there for all to see. Alongside The Beatles, Elvis Presley, Little Richard, Bruce Springsteen, The Rolling Stones, and U2 is now the name Neil Diamond. And this is what faith is about—putting your energy into someone many so-called critics consider a sideshow act and just being willing to wait it out knowing that you have cast your lot in with the real deal. I have to look back on my smirking face and just smile. If I could tell that kid in the back of the van that Neil Diamond was going to be cool enough to keep rocking into his seventies and be inducted into the Rock and Roll Hall of Fame, I would throw my Goodie comb at my future self. The old becomes new again and again and again in pop music and so should it be in the church. If we trusted the past and those so easily dismissed by the critical voices and trusted what we knew to be the real deal then perhaps faith would prove to be something more than doctrines.

## Bruce Springsteen—"Jesus Was an Only Son"

Bruce Springsteen's CD *Devils and Dust* marked the completion of a trilogy of acoustic albums dating back over twenty years to the landmark 1982 album *Nebraska* (one of my desert island discs) and the 1995 *The Ghost of Tom Joad. Devils and Dust* roams around the Southwest border lands of the US and seems haunted by the liminal space betwixt and between languages—songs weaving together Spanish and English like a Cormac McCarthy novel. What makes Springsteen such an interesting figure in American popular music is his ability to draw on the everyman experience and make it an anthem for the masses—a rock-and-roll version of Aaron Copland's *Fanfare for the Common Man.*

When he was inducted into the Rock and Roll Hall of Fame, Bono gave the induction speech and put it this way regarding Springsteen's appeal:

> He didn't buy the mythology that screwed so many people. Instead he created an alternate mythology, one where ordinary lives became extraordinary and heroic. Bruce Springsteen feels familiar to us. But it's not an easy familiarity, is it? Even his band seems to stand taller when he walks in the room. It's complex. He's America's writer, and critic. It's like in *Badlands*, he's Martin Sheen and Terrence Mallick. To be so accessible and so private. . . . But then again, he is an Irish-Italian, with a Jewish-sounding name. What more do you want?[18]

Central to this "alternate mythology" for Springsteen is the desire to escape and the sense that we are all—to use the title of his breakthrough album—*Born to Run*. In an interview with *Creem* magazine back in 1978, Springsteen discussed how rock and roll provided that sense of escape:

> Rock and roll came to my house where there seemed to be no way out. It seemed like a dead-end street, nothing I liked to do, nothing I wanted to do, except roll over and go to sleep or something. And it came into my house—snuck in, ya know, and opened up a whole world of possibilities. Rock and roll. The Beatles opened doors. Ideally, if any stuff I do could ever do that for somebody, that's the best rock and roll motivates. It's the big, gigantic motivator; at least it was for me.[19]

In this way, music became religion, a means of absolution and release, for Bruce Springsteen in the way that it has for many Americans who feel that the church says nothing and that a four-minute pop song understands and speaks to the core of their deepest needs.

18. Bono, "Bono on Bruce Springsteen."
19. Marsh, *Bruce Springsteen: Two Hearts*, 86.

Springsteen grew up Catholic, attending grammar school at St. Rose of Lima at the corner of South Street Lincoln Place in Freehold, New Jersey. Commenting on his song "Jesus Was an Only Son" on a recent *VH1 Storytellers* episode, he said, "Once you have been introduced to Golgotha, you are haunted by it forever."[20] Organized religion is a subject of disdain for Springsteen. This is easily understood in the light of his reflections on parochial schooling. In one interview he reflects on his time at St. Rose of Lima this way:

> In the third grade a nun stuffed me into a garbage can she kept under her desk because she told me that's where I belonged. . . . I hated school. I had the big hate. I remember one time, I was in eighth grade and I wised off and they sent me down to the first class and made me sit in these little desks, you know, little chairs. And the sister, she said, "Show this young man what we do to people who smile in this classroom"—I was probably laughing at being sent down there. And this kid, this six-year-old who has no doubt been taught to do this, he comes over to me—him standing up and me sitting in this little desk are about eye-to-eye—and he slams me in the face. I can still feel the sting. I was in shock.[21]

Yet even with this disdain for organized religion, Bruce Springsteen continues to expand on the God-haunted longing of the everyman in his "alternate mythology" for America. This is particularly true in "Jesus was an Only Son," from the album *Devils and Dust*.

> In the garden at Gethsemane
> He prayed for the life he'd never live,
> He beseeched his Heavenly Father to remove
> The cup of death from his lips
>
> Now there's a loss that can never be replaced,
> A destination that can never be reached,
> A light you'll never find in another's face,
> A sea whose distance cannot be breached.

Even though we are "born to run," there is still something of that "loss that can never be replaced, a destination that can never be reached," that seeks for the face of God throughout Bruce Springsteen's music. It is good to see the searching and the authentic questioning continue onward.

20. Springsteen and Diomedi. *VH1 Storytellers: Springsteen*, tracks 11 and 12.
21. Masur, *Runaway Dream*, 120.

# 3

# Hope

ONE OF THE MARKS of the 2008 presidential race was the way in which America came to a renewed interest in a very old word: hope. Both Democrats and Republicans pointed to the new millennium as a time for hope. After the crises of the Columbine shootings, the 9/11 attacks, the continued wars in the Middle East, and the sense of dread about the economy, what it meant to hope became a politically contested issue. What do we place our hope in? What is there worth hoping for? As we have looked at the various ways in which pop music has framed how sonic mystics think about and experience faith, we now turn our attention to this virtue of hope. For many people, to have hope is to have a hold of something that is beyond present experience. Some Christians for example will speak of hope in terms of the afterlife and what heaven represents, as a place and time far away from earthly struggles; for them to hope is to hold onto the promise that the afterlife will be better than the one we are living now. In theological studies this constitutes a domain of study called *eschatology*—the study of the last or final things. To have a promise in a better tomorrow certainly seems like a good way to go, but a focus on what is yet to come isn't worth much if it doesn't offer some way to affect our lives in the here and now.

One contemporary thinker who has helped the Christian church reimagine its understanding of hope is the German theologian Jürgen Moltmann. In his seminal work *Theology of Hope*, Moltmann challenges us to remember that eschatology is not a statement of possibility alone but an affirmation of promise in the reality of hope as it takes up residence in the here and now, as the foundation of what we mean by faith. As he states, "faith takes its stand on hope and 'hastens beyond this world' [as noted by John Calvin]. [Calvin] did not mean by this that Christian faith flees the world, but he did mean that it strains after the future. To believe does in fact mean to cross and transcend bounds, to be engaged in an exodus. Yet this happens in a way that does not suppress or skip the unpleasant realities."[1] To be hopeful as Moltmann describes is to be straining for the promise of the Not Yet amidst the "unpleasant reality" of our current context and then returning that promise palpably into the way we live and move and have our being.

This is the way many pop songs try to get at what it means to hope as well. Sure, there are the sugary sweet songs that have a Pollyannic frame to the world and only offer a momentary distraction from real life. These songs have the spiritual nutritional value of Pop Tarts and as such you will not be finding songs like "MMMBop" by Hanson in this section. The detractors who speak in unilateral terms regarding pop music being all flash and no substance will hold that pop music is merely one candy-coated "MMMBop" track after another and therefore offers nothing in the way of alleviating the world's suffering nor pointing us toward a worthy tomorrow. For these detractors there are volumes of songs to choose from to support this view. That said, just as not every human being is the embodiment of the *American Pie* movie franchise, so not every pop song's pathway to hope is void of depth or transcendence. Conversely, not every song sold in the CCM market portrays a picture of hope that is worthy of the gospel to which it appeals nor the person of Jesus who often gets a shout out.

So what are some of the ways that hope is being sung about in our neighbor's hymnal? How do sonic mystics think about hope based on what is on shuffle play on their MP3 player? As theologian Darrell Guder challenges us, we are to see our lives as

> developmental and dynamic in nature, if we believe the church is the work of the creating and inspiring Spirit of God and is moving toward God's promised consummation of all things. *Neither the church nor its interpretive doctrine may be static.* New biblical insights will convert the church and its theology; new historical challenges will raise questions never before considered; and new

1. Moltmann, *Theology of Hope*, 19.

cultural contexts will require a witnessing response that redefines
how we function.[2]

To this end perhaps the church can add some new songs of hope gleaned
from our neighbor's hymnal that can redefine not only how the church
thinks of hope, but of the artists and sonic mystics who have an aspect of
hope that we all can benefit from.

### Aimee Mann—"Save Me"

Where pop music is filled with a cast of characters both soaringly heroic
and woefully tragic who haven't a hope in the world, there is also a significant yet often overlooked population who are high functioning yet per-
petually lost souls that inhabit the nether region between living happily
ever after and giving up entirely. To put it another way, some people are
merely mundane freaks and geeks who are just painfully average. Often
the question of hope gets discussed on the extreme ends of the human
spectrum—either we have found everything we have ever desired and are
finally at rest or we simply collapse and turn to ashes amidst our misery.
While this is the experience of some people, it is not the experience of
many others, such as the person who has the average job that isn't horrible and yet isn't amazing, who has children who aren't perfect, whose
marriage has moments that are celebratory and yet long stretches where
the discussions never go further than paying bills, watering the plants,
and taking out the trash. For the painfully average and mundane, there is
always the sense that something has to give, that we were meant for something more, something great, someone who really understands us in ways
that we don't even understand ourselves. Yet if we cannot resolve these
massive existential questions, then perhaps giving up is the option, to stop
swimming upstream, to cease the striving for something more and simply
free-fall into whatever pit we have been fearing we would descend into if
we simply stopped trying so hard. For the painfully average and mundane,
Aimee Mann provides a soundtrack to this longing to move beyond the
wallowing and wondering about something or someone more.

Mann's career took off in the 1980s, like so many artists of that decade, in large part due to the explosion of MTV and the music video. Her
band 'Til Tuesday was a regular fixture on this new media outlet, and
her quirky lyrics coupled with pop sensible hooks whilst sporting spiked

2. Guder, "Missional Church," 12; emphasis added.

hair with a bleached rat-tail and twelve-hole Doc Marten boots made her the perfect video darling. Like a pop music Goldilocks, she wasn't too pushy and in-your-face nor was she too introspective and appealing only to introverted singer-songwriter types but hitting a perfect pop middle of "just right," offering complex aspects of what it means to be human with the pop sensibility of the masses. 'Til Tuesday's big single, "Voices Carry," was a song of disillusionment with a relationship as the protagonist of the song is being pressured to compromise and turn into a person she is not. In the video, Aimee Mann is being transformed by her boyfriend's expectations into the personification of what in the 1980s would be termed a Yuppie (young urban professional) who is consumed with image but shallow in substance—putting away the ideals of the struggling artist and embracing the values of Wall Street and Madison Avenue. In a moment of art imitating life, this scenario in "Voices Carry" mirrors the struggle that Aimee Mann faced early in her career. While the single "Voices Carry" won Best Video of the Year in 1985 and the album performed well, 'Til Tuesday struggled with their next two releases and Mann eventually went solo in the early 1990s.

Rather than try to bend herself into a songwriter for the typical sullen jilted girlfriend in the suburbs that was expected after "Voices Carry," Mann instead embraced characters in her songs who were not so mainstream—odd figures who as misfits to the world of status quo found life difficult yet had integrity and were willing to admit to life's pain and sorrow as much as its joys. This cast of characters came into its clearest focus with the release of the soundtrack to the 1999 Paul Thomas Anderson film *Magnolia* and her 2002 album *Bachelor No. 2*. Songs like "Wise Up," "Drive Sideways," and "Save Me" quietly sang from the margins of the mainstream and gave voice to the odd and different who weren't on MTV videos or gracing the covers of *Cosmopolitan* or *Elle*. These were average people, going to work on the bus or subway, doing entry-level work and returning to dark apartments to watch television alone until exhaustion took hold. There were no knights in shining armor riding in to save the day nor was there a cataclysmic event to take control of the situation and end it all once and for all. While the days bleed one to another, there is always some hope lurking at the background for Mann's cast of freaks and geeks. Whether it is the voice of a choir that gives support to the characters in "Wise Up" or the ability to even ask for someone to "save me," Mann's characters offer a no-nonsense, unflinching look at the mundane and trivial lives so many people inhabit and acknowledges them for what they are—lives that will never be the stuff of epic poems or Nobel prizes, but still lives that dimly refract moments of hope enough to wake up each day, shake off the stupor, and set their feet walking yet again. Central to this hope, which is most clearly seen and heard in "Save Me," is that it is not truly hope if it isn't first forged in the hope to love and be loved in return. Rather than seeking fame and wealth as a way out of our lives of mundane striving, there is always the possibility that love

> will come to save me
> C'mon and save me
> If you could save me
> From the ranks of the freaks
> Who suspect they could never love anyone.

What is often the mistake of many of the big megachurch models of Christianity is the idea that an encounter with God is always something so cataclysmic as to blow your life apart stem to stern like a hurricane. So people wait and wait and wait for the big bang to strike them from on high and all the while cease living, let alone loving. The fact remains that many people do not experience life this way and are left wondering what they have been doing wrong. For Aimee Mann's characters, akin to God appearing to Elijah in 1 Kings 19, meaning and purpose is not to be found in the crash and bang of lightning from on high all the time. In fact, for many of the "freaks who suspect that they could never love anyone" it will come in a still, small voice of promise and patience tested in the act of believing that love is possible and worth risking even to the point of having one's heart broken once again. In the courage to ask sincerely that someone save us and letting people know that we desire to love, we find that love is possible because we admit that our desire to love and be loved is part of what hope is all about. In this way, perhaps the freaks that Aimee Mann sings about, who we might see as average and mundane people, are actually living out the epic life of hope in our midst—not waiting for the bolt of lightning nor the burning bush nor the crash and clang of the storm before getting on with life, but just loving in spite of any massive prodding. Perhaps it will be the freaks and geeks who will be the heroes in the end.

## The Killers—"All These Things That I've Done"

One of most famous engagements with secular culture on the part of the church was when the Apostle Paul challenged the Athenians to look around their culture and see the ways God was speaking to them. As Paul says in Acts 17:27, we can find evidence of God in our culture if we're alert. Reasoning with many of the urbane thinkers of Athens, Paul noted that many of the things that they held as being purely secular and only of human creation were actually pointing their attention to the Creator of all things. The question is whether we are willing to explore this as a possibility—that perhaps what gives a painting beauty is something more than the painter and what gives a song its transcendence is even beyond the skill of a the performer. Perhaps, muses Paul, there is a grander work happening in culture and that even in so-called secular society God is poking through. "God did this so that people would seek him," says Paul, "and perhaps reach out for him and find him, though he is not far from each one of us." This is a message of hope to be sure and an encouragement to look deeper into the things that fill our lives with joy and meaning and to have the courage to ask whether the deep joy we experience in music is because it ultimately points beyond itself and to something much deeper and more profound.

Highly sought-after record producer T-Bone Burnett, who is also a Christian, may have said it best years ago: "If Jesus is the Light of the World, there are two kinds of songs you can write. You can write songs about the light, or you can write songs about what you can see from the light. That's what I try to do. A bricklayer's job is to build a good wall that will stand against the rain and wind. Writing JESUS on it isn't going to help it withstand the storms."[3] Sometimes music points us to the love in Christ, and sometimes the light of God through popular music exposes us to the despair, anger, and hopelessness found in contemporary culture that needs redeeming.

One example is "All These Things That I've Done," from The Killers' debut album "Hot Fuzz." The Killers could certainly raise some eyebrows and cause people to wonder if anything good could come from a band of peppy glam rockers. But this song keeps with the Christian tradition of lament that points toward hope. Singer Brandon Flowers sounds like the psalmist as he pleads for the ability to "stand up," and "let go," and for the

3. Turner, *Hungry for Heaven*, 165.

"direction to perfection," ending with a simple "help me out." As the song reaches its end, Flowers lays down everything in this gospel service:

> Over and out, last call for sin
> While everyone's lost, the battle is won
> With all these things that I've done, all these things that I've done
> If you can hold on . . . hold on.

The question left to the listener is whether we can "hold on," or are we willing to let go of that which binds us, restricts us, and move into a life of grace now that "the battle is won"? "All These Things That I've Done" is not unique in its ability to highlight truth in a fashion that some in the church might dismiss as we have seen throughout this book. So the question remains, where is the light shining in the music you are listening to these days? Like the Apostle Paul in Acts 17, let us be a generation ready to assert that God is indeed evident in pop culture, and that "God did this so that people would seek him and perhaps reach out for him and find him, though he is not far from each one of us."

## The Replacements—"Here Comes a Regular"

When I entered graduate school, I suppose in the back of my mind I held the notion that being a theologian was something akin to what Lloyd Dobler, the great antihero for 1980s romantic geeks in Cameron Crowe's *Say Anything*, played by John Cusack, termed a "dare to be great" situation. I shared Dobler's great vocational manifesto: "I don't want to sell anything, buy anything, or process anything as a career. I don't want to sell anything bought or processed, or buy anything sold or processed, or process anything sold, bought, or processed, or repair anything sold, bought, or processed. You know, as a career, I don't want to do that."[4] In short, I thought that being a teacher and researcher of theology was such a venture. True, idealism has to shake hands with realism from time to time, but lately I have found that this handshake has become an arm wrestling match. Like any academic discipline, theology is the cast from an alternative universe of *It's a Wonderful Life* with starry-eyed George Bailey visionaries and cranky old Mr. Potter-type curmudgeons presenting papers side-by-side in the academic conference version of *Bedford Falls*. These typologies may be extremes, but like many aphorisms and

4. Crowe, *Say Anything*.

clichés, they do arise from somewhere and often times that somewhere is the here and now.

I had thought that I would hold fast to the promise I made in seminary before heading off to do my PhD in Scotland—that I was one of many who would seek to reflect theologically on those things that Paul Tillich called "ultimate concerns" and let those questions form and change the way I was living in the world, not only as an academic, but as a follower of Christ. I balked at the notion of merely repeating tired rhetoric, aping safe phrases from safe theologians of old in order to nuzzle up to the world of the high academic discourse. In short, with a wink and a nod to Rickard Dawkins, the last thing I wished to be known as was yet another "theological meme machine." To even suggest giving in to such banality was to be met with an echo of Lloyd Dobler's folk-singing best friend Corey Flood in *Say Anything*: "That'll never be me, that'll never be me. That'll never be, never be me. NO! . . . NO, NEVER, NEVER, EVER! And don't you EVER THINK IT!"

Fast-forward to today. I have just left a lecture on liturgical and sacramental theology and as I reflect on my lecture notes delivered to this class of undergraduates I am shocked by how . . . dare I say it . . . "sold, bought, and processed" these lecture notes really are. Where is the sense of radical engagement, the sense of pushing boundaries and getting to the "ultimate concern" that is at the heart of the Eucharist? What happened?

I started to reflect on these questions as I watched my daughter run around our living room with The Replacements singing in the background. The Replacements (known to many of their fans as "the Mats") arose out of the "Liverpool of the Mid-West," Minneapolis, Minnesota (with Hüsker Dü and Prince sharing neighboring zip codes) at a time in the mid-1980s when Ronald Reagan and George Bush Sr. were fresh on the scene and the film and Brat Pack of *St. Elmo's Fire* made Washington, DC, into a cool college town. Headed up by lead vocalist and songwriter Paul Westerberg, along with bassist Tommy Stinson, guitarist Bob Stinson, and drummer Chris Mars, The Replacements stand as one of the truly seminal American garage-punk bands to come out of the "decade of excess" that was the American 80s, and Paul Westerberg can be argued to be one of the best rock-and-roll songwriters since Elvis Costello. In an interview, Westerberg said that "I think the marriage of honesty and melody are my two main things. If I'm short in one suit, then I try to overcompensate with the other. It has to be one of those two for me to be truly interesting."[5] The fact that this is the focus of a rock-and-roll songwriter probably isn't too surprising. Rather, what is surprising is the fact this vision isn't evident in the writing and practice of what passes as theology today. Hope is about shouting "here comes a regular" so that the marginalized and forsaken know that they haven't been forgotten and letting our theology become something that raises a glass in their name. As I watched my daughter dance around the living room to a song Westerberg wrote reminding us that people are not to be forgotten, I was reminded what theology should be about and it is providing hope for the folks Westerberg sings about—the marginalized who just want to be remembered as "regulars." Hopefully you will find this the case as well.

### Kanye West—"Jesus Walks"

In his book *Why White Kids Love Hip Hop: Wankstas, Wiggers, Wannabes, and the New Reality of Race in America*, Bakari Kitwana makes the rather strong point that

> America, like the great empires before her, may be displaying the early warning signs of decline. The one hope of saving the country could be simply listening to our young people. Rather than the source of the problems facing American youth, hip-hop, more than anything else, has helped prepare our youth to confront not only race but some of the crises facing the nation's young people.[6]

Kanye West first rose to fame as a producer for Roc-A-Fella Records, where he eventually achieved recognition for his work on Jay-Z's album *The Blueprint*, as well as hit singles for musical artists including Alicia Keys, Ludacris, and Janet Jackson. His style of production originally used pitched-up vocal samples from soul songs incorporated with his own drums and instruments. However, subsequent productions saw him broadening his musical palette and expressing influences encompassing 70s R & B, baroque pop, trip-hop, arena rock, folk, alternative, electronica, synth-pop, and classical music.

West released his debut album *The College Dropout* in 2004, his second album *Late Registration* in 2005, his third album *Graduation* in 2007, and his fourth album *808s & Heartbreak* in 2008. His 2010 album *My*

---

5. Cited by Gluck, "Love Untold: St. Paul's Letters to the Philistines."

6. Kitwana, *Why White Kids Love Hip-Hop*, 10.

*Beautiful Dark Twisted Fantasy* topped many of critic's lists as one of the albums of the year if not the decade.

His father is Ray West, a former Black Panther who was one of the first black photojournalists at the *Atlanta Journal-Constitution*, and is now a Christian counselor. West's mother, Dr. Donda West, was a professor of English at Clark Atlanta University and the chair of the English department at Chicago State University before retiring to serve as West's manager. He was raised in a middle-class environment, attending Polaris High School in suburban Oak Lawn, Illinois, after living in Chicago.

The song is essentially a spiritual exultation, wherein West discusses how Jesus "walks" with all manner of people, from the sinner to the saint. Towards this end, the first conceptual verse of the song is told through the eyes of a drug dealer contemplating his relationship with God. It reportedly took over six months for West to draw inspiration for the second verse. West also uses the song to express his critical views on how the media seems to shy away from songs that address matters of faith, while embracing songs discussing violence, sex, and illegal drugs. He rhymes, "So here go my single, dog, radio needs this / They say you can rap about anything except for Jesus / That means guns, sex, lies, video tapes / But if I talk about God my record won't get played, huh?" This is in fact directly taken from West's past experiences, where early on when he was struggling to get signed onto a record label, many executives turned him down after he played a "Jesus Walks" demo for them. Their reasoning was that he didn't conform to the stereotypes associated with mainstream hip-hop and therefore was not as marketable. Many of his friends in the music industry also warned him that while the song was fantastic, it would never make it to radio. Yet the song not only made it on the radio, but became a massive hit. Hope finds us in many ways—in the courage to be free to express our artistic vision even when we are told it won't amount to much, the willingness to find strength and conviction in a song that says Jesus chooses to walk with us even in our darkest hour, and telling the truth in and through all we do. As the protagonist of the song challenges the listener to remember, in all things hope is present where Jesus walks. And that seems to be in places both sacred and seemingly profane.

### Elliott Smith—"Miss Misery"

Portland, Oregon, is known as the "City of Roses." It is a great place that channels the vibe of other cities at opposing ends of the I-5 corridor here on the West coast of America—the beat sensibility of San Francisco and the caffeine-induced grunge introspection of Seattle—even though it is a city that sports a wonderful river walk and the temple to used book lovers that is Powell's, one of the greatest independent used bookstores on the planet. Portland used to be the lesser cousin of major cities on the West coast, until it found its hero and martyr. Today's cities become personalities when they lift up an icon that both embodies what the collective urban culture is yearning for and challenges the city's future at the same time—an artist who, for a brief time, embodies the unique urban history of a place while adding chapters to its history. New York had Lou Reed in the 1960s, Detroit had Iggy Pop from the early 70s, Seattle had Kurt Cobain in the early 90s. And Portland has Elliott Smith.

When most people think back on Elliott Smith's career, three words come to mind: *Good Will Hunting*. Gus Van Sant, a fellow Portland auteur and indie darling, featured Smith's fractured and tortured songs in the 1997 film about a genius trapped in the life of an abused, emotionally fragile Peter Pan. The movie starred then relatively unknown actors Matt Damon and Ben Affleck and catapulted Elliott Smith from the Portland indie scene to a spot on the Oscars stage next to Celine Dion. In an act that seemed to endorse Frederick Nietzsche's aphorism that "God is Dead," Celine Dion ended up winning the Oscar that year. In many ways, if the movie had been focusing on a musical genius rather than on a mathematical wunderkind, we would have been watching *Good Elliott Smith* on the screen. Elliott Smith's music came at a time when the Pacific Northwest grunge mania was finally dying out and his brand of "miniaturized psychodrama" seemed the ideal balm for a regional music scene that felt as if it had just been taken apart at the seams. In a retrospective article of Elliott's career, Portland writer John Graham talks about Elliott's connection to his sense of place as a Portland musician:

> Elliott's early solo albums are like cheat sheets for comprehending every Rose City songwriter who ever wrestled with a four-track recorder in his or her bedroom: Fighting the guitar for that elusive transitional bridge chord. Trying to decipher lyrics scribbled onto a bar napkin at last call. Whispering into the microphone so as not to wake the housemates. It was these confessional tales, on *Roman Candle*, *Elliott Smith* and *Either/Or*, which made him such an adored figure around town. There was something about the solo albums—so private and yet strident at the same time—that hit some kind of Portland indie-rock G-spot. Witnessing the odd

symbiosis that occurred between Elliott and his audiences during those early shows was like being privy to a cerebral orgy.[7]

Elliott Smith's music is the sound of Portland—lyrics like "They're waking you up to close the bar / The street's wet, you can tell by the sound of the cars" (from the song "Clementine") could describe Glasgow's Ashton Lane at 3 am in rainy Scotland, but it's a scene that is deeply grounded in almost every rain- and beer-soaked curb that a Portlander can identify. In "Condor Avenue," a song Smith wrote at age seventeen that later became the centerpiece for 1994's *Roman Candle*, he writes like James Joyce describing Dublin in *Ullysses*: "She took the Oldsmobile out past Condor Avenue / The fairground's lit / A drunk man sits by the gate she's driving through / Got his hat tipped back bottle back in between his teeth / Looks like he's buried in sand at the beach." Same goes for "Needle in the Hay" from Smith's self-titled 1995 album: "Now on the bus / Nearly touching this dirty retreat / Falling out 6th and Powell / A dead sweat in my teeth . . ."

I saw Elliott Smith in Glasgow at a venue called The Garage. It was one of the hottest days I ever spent in Scotland, probably eighty degrees in that crowded bar. Smith had a wool cap on and my wife, seven months pregnant with our daughter Clara, was wondering how loud was too loud for our yet to be born child. It was a great show, but he looked like one of J. M. Barrie's lost boys from *Peter Pan*, scanning the crowd during each song looking for the exit, or maybe the entrance to somewhere else.

The rest of the story regarding Elliott Smith following that Oscar-night performance next to Celine Dion is tragically basic: he gets a major contract with DreamWorks, releases a couple of great albums on a major label (*XO, Figure 8*), moves his base to LA, and eventually dies of multiple stab wounds to the heart. Whether this is a result of suicide or a homicide remains on the unsolved issues of 1990s indie rock.[8] I am sure there were psychotic issues surrounding the depression he faced, but I continue to wonder; maybe, like Dorothy in *The Wizard of Oz*, those stabs to the chest were the clicking of metaphysical ruby slippers, and maybe those whispered lo-fi lyrics were really Smith's way of saying, "there's no place like home." We can't know. But when I listen to Elliott Smith now, I think about going home, because that seems to be where Elliott wanted to go all

---

7. Graham, "Elliott Smith (1969–2003)."

8. There continues to be mystery surrounding Smith's death and debate about whether it was indeed suicide or possibly homicide. See Abramovich, "New York in Reverse," as well as Petridis, "Mysterious Death of Mr. Misery."

along. For many a sonic mystic listening to Elliott Smith and other artists whose music evokes a deep sense of longing for a place to be known and loved, the question for the church isn't necessarily how to create a place to bring them into—often times there is a longing for a place that the church will never be entirely nor was meant to be. Sometimes this longing embodied in the music of Elliott Smith and other artists like him is for a place that the church needs to go to rather than draw people away from and discover all that it has for us, a place that many people find through songs like Smith's desire—a place that takes struggle and pain seriously, a place that doesn't offer pithy answers but does offer authentic relationships. It's a place where no one has the upper hand and everyone can feel valuable and not merely like a project. The faith of Elliott Smith was in a belief that a real place like Portland could be the place where real lives can and should grow and thrive. Too often the church has desired to build a world apart from the places dreamed of and longed for in songs like Smith's and therefore holds nothing for the sonic mystic who enters the halls of homogeneity that are many modern church buildings. As opposed to drawing people into our worlds, perhaps it is time for Christians to journey to the places where sonic mystics like Smith and others are not only dreaming of, but are struggling to make sense of even as you read this sentence. As Smith longed for home and the world of success pulled him away from it, he lost himself. Maybe there is something of that story going on in the lives of many who sit in pews on a Sunday morning and wonder how they got there and dream of somewhere else—a place that they would love to go, not alone, but with someone who is open-hearted enough to find meaning and hope under their neighbor's roof and at their neighbor's table.

### Radiohead—OK Computer

As the first decade of the new millennium came to a close, top-ten lists abounded. In order to spike periodical and broadsheet sales (as well as Nielson ratings in the US to attract advertising dollars), the forming of top-ten lists is a surefire way to crunch data, opinions, and give people a clean and concise way of getting a sense of what is going on. In 2005, *Spin* magazine put out its twentieth anniversary issue and listed the top one hundred albums of 1985–2005. As a bit of a surprise, *Spin* gave top honors not to 2Pac or Nirvana, but to Radiohead for their record *OK Computer*. With this nod to greatness, it seems fitting that this book should turn its attention to the boys from Oxfordshire and their paranoid vision of things to come and things that are.

Released in 1997 to raised eyebrows and critical rants and raves, Radiohead's sonic postcard to the coming millennium *OK Computer* was certainly a departure from their earlier albums, *The Bends*, with its melancholy "Fake Plastic Trees" (a staple for ubiquitous chill-out collections), and *Pablo Honey* with its slacker army anthem "Creep." *OK Computer* fed on the angst of Y2K fears and the apocalyptic vibe of the late 90s. The bubble of the dot-com rush was beginning to rise, and the *carpe diem* worship of *techne* as a salvific balm for the God-shaped void in all of us seemed to be evident as people spent more time on the Web than in person with each other. With the conviction of a mad prophet, lead singer Thom Yorke breathed his lyrics into the cybervoid of *OK Computer* as both blessing and curse. Akin to Bruce Boxleitner's character in Disney's *TRON* (the original, not the recent sequel, where Boxleitner's TRON character is only veiled and not revealed), Thom Yorke makes more sense as the embodiment of The Police's 1981 concept album *Ghost in the Machine* than as a flesh-and-blood human and finds his salvific vocation raging from within the machine rather than merely against it. Falling somewhere in the paranoid spectrum between the vocal angst of Lindsey Buckingham's jilted lover on Fleetwood Mac's 1977 *Rumours* and director and pundit Michael Moore's everyone-is-against-us-and-they-are-coming-*now* ethos, Thom Yorke is certainly the voice of conspiracy theorists obsessed with Area 51 and grassy knolls everywhere. "Between Thom Yorke's orange-alert worldview and the band's meld of epic guitar rock and electronic glitch," wrote *Spin*'s Chuck Klosterman about choosing *OK Computer*, the album "not only forecast a decade of music but uncannily predicted our global culture of communal distress. . . . [It] manages to sound how the future will feel. . . . It's a mechanical album that always feels alive, even when its words are spoken by a robot."

There has been a rash of writing on this topic of loss of humanity amidst the technological undertow. The Gothic paranoia that what we create will ultimately destroy us is as old as Babel (Mary Shelley's *Frankenstein*, unlike the contemporary reimaginings on film, was a deeply theological treatise). Have we lost our humanity amidst our dependence on technology? Or perhaps, as in the reimagining of *Battlestar Galactica* on the Sci-Fi Channel (now Syfy), has God's favor shifted such that technology, not humanity, is now the chosen of God (i.e., Cylons are called by God to eradicate the human race)? Machines, after all, only adhere to their primary programming and are not distracted by low-hanging fruit on trees of knowledge. You can follow this line of thinking in the closing anxiety of "Paranoid Android," as God, not Elvis, is the last to leave the building of creation and humanity is abandoned not to a garden, but to a wasteland of its own tending:

> That's it, sir
> You're leaving
> The crackle of pigskin
> The dust and the screaming
> The yuppies networking
> The panic, the vomit
> The panic, the vomit
> God loves his children, God loves his children, yeah!

As an album that came out long before the world Twittered and Face-booked, *OK Computer* seems to yearn honestly for some form of answer even though the malaise of the lyrics remains doubtful of God's response or even God's return, yet the hope and faith for God is still lurking on the ends. It is unfortunate that the blow of *OK Computer*'s panic and anxiety around our increasing need for technology has been softened by films like *Dark City*, *The Matrix*, and *Inception*—films that provide easy answers before the big questions can take hold and challenge us to our core.

More than a decade after its release, *OK Computer* has legs to run and is certainly worth listening to again. As Radiohead has continued speaking into the anxiety of technological isolation with releases like *Hail to the Thief, Kid A, In Rainbows*, and *The King of Limbs*, it is a testimony to its artistry that jazz artists like Brad Mehldau will cover "Exit Music for a Film" off *OK Computer*. When was the last time a jazz artist took on a rock song rather than the other way around? For the sonic mystic listening to Radiohead, the journey isn't one of pure despair in the face of neither technology nor paralyzing fear. Where much of the evangelical subculture has chosen to either embrace every latest technological innovation without question as a desperate nod to relevancy or dismiss any use of technology since the Guttenberg press as a distraction from the truth of the gospel, Radiohead offers another way. As pop artists like Radiohead engage the various technological innovations that can shape their music, they speak into the anxiety and fears of the generation by imagining a world into existence within a pop song where fear never has the last word and the subject of concern is not social networking platforms, but the hopes, dreams, and loves of the people who are shaped by these technological innovations for good and for ill. Where many Christians worry about technology, Radiohead has faith in human beings and the power of love to be the last word long after the lights on the computer screen grow dim. True, this is not the saving love of Christ overtly spoken of in the Gospels, but it is a hopefulness amidst the age of anxiety that still has a voice that pleads and hopes amidst the machines that could be a way of doing faith anew.

### Sufjan Stevens—"Casimir Pulaski Day"

I always knew that Steve Martin was a prophet when I would listen to that scratched *Let's Get Small* album in the 1970s. In this case I am thinking of his prophetic utterance in his stand-up routine entitled "Grandmother's Song" where he says, "You can't sing anything sad on a banjo."

There is something in the American ethos when a banjo kicks in that evokes either gothic dread (think "Dueling Banjos" in *Deliverance*) or some untouched innocence that speaks of a bygone state of grace. (Imagine Alexander Pope's noble savage from his 1734 "Essay on Man" pickin' and a-grin' and you'll get the picture.) Banjos continue to make their way into pop music even beyond the usual alt-country trend to see banjos as the natural grandparent to a Flying V guitar. One notable example can be found on the CD/DVD edition of U2's *How to Dismantle an Atomic Bomb* and the version of "Vertigo (Temple Bar Mix)" that has Edge playing solo banjo. In short, banjos are just cool, and the latest indie wunderkind to embrace the banjo is Sufjan Stevens, whose albums *Illinoise* (also called, in a nice tongue-in-cheek nod to Quiet Riot, *Come On Feel the Illinoise*), *All Delighted People*, and *The Age of Adz* take the banjo to places both strange and heartwarming.

For a time, Sufjan certainly was the "What? You haven't heard *him* yet?" artist of the moment in indie circles and on the blogosphere. His epic attempt to record albums based on all fifty states (he had recorded *Michigan* prior to *Illinoise*) made for good PR and a nice quirky hook for rock journalists ("Will *Delaware* be an EP?" "Is there *any* music to describe *South Dakota*, and if so, why bother?"). *Seattle Weekly* described *Illinoise* as

> like a kid's 50-state book, TBS's *Portrait of America* specials from the '80s, or Rick Smolan's 24/7 coffee-table book series, *Illinoise* is

a grand, corny gesture toward painting the essence of a state with the broadest of strokes. Stevens respects both the megaopolis of Chicago and the wee village of Birds, ponders the Columbian Exposition of 1893, gets a visit from Carl Sandburg in a dream, and remembers Satchmo and Gacy and Douglas and Lincoln and Lincoln's wife. The references to stuff like the Chickenmobile and Octave Chanute might even leave Illinoisans feeling like strangers to their own state.[9]

While the subjects of Sufjan's consideration, particularly on *Michigan* and *Illinoise*, are ostensibly secular, the face of the Divine is truly alit and seeking our attention through the "bars of his rhyme." To listen to "Sufjan minimalism" is to face our hopes and fears without clutter and the knowledge that we are certainly not alone. It is hard to imagine someone as deeply devout as Sufjan Stevens in trying to bring together real life with real hope and faith in the transcendent nature of things. God is there in the background of most of Sufjan Stevens's songs. As he sings of the young friend he prays for as she dies from cancer, of the runners on the underground railroad who've "got a better life coming," of humble Decatur as "The Great I Am," God is there. As several songs blur together the patriotic declarations of a state song and merge into Blakean vision—"Peoria! Destroyia! Infinity! Divinity!" God is there emptying out our preconceived notions, illuminating our path and uniting us with a new future, a new community and a God we have never met before or only thought we did.

"Casimir Pulaski Day," on *Illinoise*, is an example of Sufjan's wrestling with the tension of belief coupled with doubt and discouragement. "Tuesday night at the Bible study / We lift our hands and we pray over your body / But nothing ever happens." The struggles of being in Bible study after Bible study and hoping upon hope that God will heal and "nothing ever happens" is certainly part of the bumpy topography of every Christian sojourner's map of life. Rather than reconcile this issue through reasoned pronouncements or blithe appeal to dogma, Sufjan lets the paradox possible in music exist as is without moralism or pity response. Amidst the strain of the faithful praying in honest unison, the voice of the banjo plunks away in the background. Rather than sound like a bad parody of *Hee Haw*, Sufjan uses a brass arrangement to counterpoint the plunking banjo voice of the humans in prayer, trumpets and trombone like a Salvation Army band giving hope to dampened urban

9. Daddino, "That Great State."

dwellers rushing from one street corner to the next on Christmas Eve. For Sufjan, two of the most unlikely instruments—the mundane banjo and the angelic instrument of choice, the trumpet—exalt each other and draw the voices of the gathered into worship *à la* The Polyphonic Spree:

> Oh the glory that the Lord has made
> And the complications when I see His face
> In the morning in the window
> Oh the glory when he took our place
> But He took my shoulders and He shook my face
> And He takes and He takes and He takes.

No matter how mundane life may seem to be, Stevens sees the story of life as a love story between himself and Jesus, God born human, a man stung and mocked and wrestled with. This has certainly carried forward into his *The Age of Adz* project released in 2010. We may see ourselves as members of a state or a country. There may be a kind of equality in a state of sin. But we are brought to an even greater unity when we love Jesus, who brings us into the highest relationship with God. For some, the Christian subtext to Sufjan Stevens's music is just not important—the themes of humanity are so clear and compelling that the music has found a large audience. Whether they believe in God the way someone sitting in a traditional pew might is not important. For the sonic mystics who are fans of Sufjan Stevens, the framing of faith is found in the sound of a banjo and a brass band coming together in a prayer service where simple answers are just too small for the God who is showing up.

### John Lennon—"Imagine"

New Year's Eve in Times Square—one of the most iconic places to be for ringing in the New Year. As the ball begins to descend on the thousands huddled together in the street at the one-minute countdown, the hope of the new year is framed by one of the most popular songs in recent history: "Imagine there's no Heaven. . . . It's easy if you try . . ." For the past few years, New Year's in Times Square has begun with an ode to imagining a new future. What is it we are hoping for?

"Imagine there's no Beatles, imagine no iconic movies, no *White Album*, no poetry books, no drawings," wrote Linda Winer for *Newsday* after panning the debut of the new Broadway musical, *Ballad of John and Yoko*, drawn from John Lennon's writings. "Then imagine there's no son before Sean, no mistress named May Pang, no deep depression, nothing really serious with drugs." As Linda Winer and others have pointed out in this most recent reimagining of John Lennon's life through art, this production is very "Ono-centric." Passing quickly over Lennon's career in the Beatles, the production gives little time to his first marriage or to the son he fathered before he met Yoko Ono. It also omits his affair that forced the couple apart for more than a year.

But when has the omission of so-called "facts" or the bending of time ever stopped people from embracing a hero of mythic stature? As much as folks try to "get real" with regard to our mythic icons, the myth and that which gave it to us will still prevail. John Lennon may have been a cheat and a jerk, but there's still one undeniable fact: he was John *freakin' Lennon*.

The Beatles and its component parts of John, Paul, George, and (yes) Ringo continue to be one of the greatest cultural influences in Western culture, hands down. Granted, John worked hard in later years to separate himself from the Beatles in interviews, but essentially the parts and the whole merged beyond separation, one of pop music's best exponents of *perichoresis*—the theological term used to describe the divine dance of Father, Son, and Holy Spirit, who maintain both their distinctiveness and yet are bound as one in unity and truth. Testimony to this fact was the release of *The Beatles: Rock Band* game and the recent addition of the Beatles' entire back catalog to the iTunes store—as the generations encounter John Lennon anew in the digital age, he will always be tied firmly to the Beatles as both a game avatar and musician.

Frankly, it is difficult to "imagine" pop music as we know it without the ghostly presence of John Lennon lurking behind the scenes, and not just because of the shape of his art but also because of the shape of his epic life: humble UK art student turned Hamburg indie musician turned megastar turned gunned-down hero of flower children around the world, a man who turned the Dakota Hotel and Mark Chapman into cultural icons in their own right. If there is a taproot from which our current understanding of pop music draws its strength, John Lennon would seem to be a good candidate.

In the arena of Christian critics, John Lennon thought a lot about Christianity and wasn't short on words in regard to where the state of the union is. "Christianity will go," said Lennon in his now-classic statement in an airport in 1966. "It will vanish and shrink. I needn't argue about that. I'm right and will be proved right. [The Beatles are] more popular than

Jesus now; I don't know which will go first, rock 'n' roll or Christianity. Jesus was all right, but it was his disciples that were ordinary. It's them twisting it [the story of Jesus] that ruins it for me."[10] Lennon's statement is something I still hear pop up from friends who feel Lennon understood something the church never has.

I do think Lennon is right to some extent. After the media backlash and the bonfires at youth retreats fueled by burning copies of *Rubber Soul*, Lennon responded by saying, "Look, I wasn't saying the Beatles are better than God or Jesus. I said 'Beatles' because it's easy for me to talk about Beatles. I could have said TV or the cinema, motor cars or anything popular and I would have gotten away with it."[11] To be honest, as we stand some forty years after these comments perhaps it is time to take Lennon seriously and not merely dismiss his comments.

Maybe the vector Lennon should have taken, rather than saying that there are a lot of things more popular than Christianity, was what he would later frame in his signature post-Beatles song, "Imagine": that the problem with religion today has more to do with a lack of imagination than with a drive for certainty.

> Imagine there's no heaven, It's easy if you try,
> No hell below us, Above us only sky,
> Imagine all the people
> living for today . . .
> Imagine there's no countries,
> It isn't hard to do,
> Nothing to kill or die for,
> No religion too,
> Imagine all the people
> living life in peace . . .

It is a moving song with a piano track that gets me every time. I have never embraced Lennon's neo-Marxist utopianism, the idea that humanity is infinitely perfectible, that meaning is purely found on an imminent plane; and "love is all you need" seems downright glib coming from a guy who could afford to spend the rest of his life staring at his navel if he wanted to, thanks to the royalty checks filling his bank account daily from "Love Me Do." But the song still gets me. I suppose it is my own lack of imagination that stirs under the weight of Lennon's tune—the fact that

10. Cleave, "How Does a Beatle Live?," quoted in Gould, *Can't Buy Me Love*, 308.

11. Ibid.

we live in an age of unbridled horrors against the poor and marginalized that never seem to abate. Perhaps Lennon's honesty in the final verse, the prayer of unity, is what gets me in the same way the end of *It's a Wonderful Life* gets me every Christmas:

> You may say I'm a dreamer,
> but I'm not the only one,
> I hope someday you'll join us,
> And the world will live as one.

That we aren't the only ones dreaming of a better today and a hope for tomorrow—like George Bailey in the big sing-along of Burns's "Auld Lang Syne"—is a drippy utopian statement, but there's something to it. And maybe that's where we begin.

## U2—"All Because of You"

Over the years, from what began with *War* and *The Unforgettable Fire* and became clarified to laser precision in *The Joshua Tree* and *Achtung Baby*, the Irish band U2 has wrestled with the twinned "angels of their better nature": (1) lyrically writing and rewriting the ways in which desire will only be fully consummated with our embrace by and with God, and (2) sustaining a distinctly musical signature that is the "U2 sound" that draws the very best from all genres to embody their music. In short: the rock-and-roll search for what theologians call *perichorisis*—the grafting together of the mystical and the carnal—body and spirit—into an incarnational face by which we can be encountered. If the early albums (*War* and *The Unforgettable Fire*) have been about *kerygma*—getting the word out—and the later albums have been about the musical form of that kerygmatic vision (*Achtung Baby*, *Zooropa*, *Pop*), then the music and creative output of the band as they enter the new millennium is about putting it all together. Many critics and fans alike heaped praise upon their 2000 release *All That You Can't Leave Behind* (*ATYCLB*) as the best U2 album since *The Joshua Tree*—I think they may want to rewrite those reviews in light of *How to Dismantle an Atomic Bomb* (*HTDAAB*) and *No Line on the Horizon* (*NLOTH*).

As many U2 fans are aware, the central theme of *HTDAAB* is so basic that it is profound: as the Beatle's succinctly put it, "all you need is love." Where *War* and *The Unforgettable Fire* made direct statements of social responsibility and railed against the political and corporate machines that were crushing people right and left through a variety of systematic evils, the more mature and even better informed Bono has come to grips not only with the magnitude of the world's woes, but has come to rest in a peace about what the silver bullet is—"give love a chance." The story goes that Bono asked Christian songwriter Michael W. Smith if he knew how one could dismantle an atomic bomb. After replying that he didn't, Bono simply answered, "Love. With love." And this is what U2 has given us in *HTDAAB*—an eleven-song intimate exposition that explores the relationship of love between humanity and God ("Vertigo," "All Because of You," "Yahweh"), parent and child ("Sometimes You Can't Make It on Your Own," "Original of the Species"), husband and wife ("City of Blinding Lights," "A Man and a Woman") and those that Christ would call our neighbors ("Miracle Drug," "Love and Peace or Else").

From *Rattle and Hum* through *Achtung Baby* and *Pop* the band that is U2 has worked with different musical pallets trying to match colors with context—blues and R&B, Europop, retro disco, and electronica— all the various hues of the day. Yet trying to chase after the proverbial musical zeitgeist is akin to chasing after the wind—in many ways what *HTDAAB* seems to embody is a bit of the rest and repose that comes after a career forged by trying to graft spirit and body together. Like Job in the final chapter, Bono seemed ready in his "desert" phases of *The Joshua Tree* (mystical desert) and *Pop* (urban collapse) to resign and empty himself out before God—"I had heard of You by the hearing of the ear, but now my eye sees You; therefore I despise myself, and repent in dust and ashes" (Job 42: 5, 6)—and take whatever is to come, as we heard in his duet with Johnny Cash in "The Wanderer" that capped off *Zooropa*—"Yeah, I went with nothing, nothing but the thought of you. I went wandering." But the years after *Zooropa* and *Pop* for Bono have been filled with a rebirth of his bent toward the social gospel only glimpsed at during the mid-80s and his now famous cry in Band Aid's "Do They Know It's Christmas?"—"Thank God it's them and not you."

Over the past decade, audiences and intentional conversations with some of the greatest living activists, economists, and political leaders of the twentieth and twenty-first centuries—Desmond Tutu, Nelson Mandela, Pope John Paul II, Mother Teresa, etc.—have forged a vision for Bono that has made overcoming debt for developing countries a mandate for his life. Taking seriously the commission of Leviticus 25:10—"Proclaim liberty throughout the lands and to all the inhabitants thereof, it shall be a jubilee for you"—the Drop the Debt, End Aids Now, and Jubilee 2000 campaigns galvanized a vision of responsive activism that was constructive rather than merely retaliatory. Yet after the smoke cleared, the honorary doctorates bestowed, the confrontations with US and other First World leaders, Bono seems to have unclenched his fists and resigned himself to truthfully answering the question that has been nagging his musical search since "I Will Follow," the first song on U2's first album *Boy*:

> I was on the outside when you said
> You needed me
> I was looking at myself
> I was blind, I could not see.
> I was on the inside
> When they pulled the four walls down
> I was looking through the window
> I was lost, I am found.

What does it mean to follow—and what do we desire through it all? Faith is a question posed to us more than it is an answer, and at its most fundamental level the question is whether we will follow or not regardless of circumstances, certainty or the lack thereof. Faith as following is something sonic mystics embody in the way they experience music and the communities within which they find themselves. This life of faith as following is explored throughout the U2 canon and in *HTDAAB* seems to be simply this: the life of faith is to follow the love of God to wherever and whomever that journey takes us and we are to love fully and completely those we meet along the way. In short, U2 comes full circle in this album by resting in the assurance that, all in all, it all comes down to love. Yet this is not a pop-psych sort of love even though it is housed in a pop song. In "Miracle Drug" the teenager in "I Will Follow" grows up and embraces the fullness of love found in God and poured out on others:

> God I need your help tonight
> Beneath the noise
> Below the din
> I hear a voice
> It's whispering
> In science and in medicine
> "I was a stranger
> You took me in"
> The songs are in your eyes
> I see them when you smile

> I've had enough of romantic love
> I'd give it up, yeah, I'd give it up.

In "All Because of You," there is a comfort in merely being made alive and living in a way that doesn't have to strive or prove anything beyond praise:

> I saw you in the curve of the moon
> In the shadow cast across my room
> You heard me in my tune
> When I just heard confusion
> All because of you
> All because of you
> All because of you
> I am . . . I am.

The closing tracks of U2 albums always seem to close as benedictions and "songs of sending" of sorts—an overt turn to the liturgical and direct assessment of Christendom and the Christ that can be lost amidst it. Whether it is the direct Biblicism of "40" from *War*, the mystical apophatic darkness of "Love is Blindness" from *Achtung Baby* ("Love is drowning in a deep well / All the secrets, and no one to tell"), the reframing of *Pilgrim's Progress* for the Twitter and Facebook generation in "The Wanderer" from *Zooropa*, the whispering cry of the psalmist in "Wake Up Dead Man" from *Pop*, or the resignation to the call of "Grace" ("What once was hurt / What once was friction / What left a mark / No longer stings / Because Grace makes beauty / Out of ugly things / Grace makes beauty out of ugly things") from ATYCLB, U2 continues to draw its productions to a close with an opening to something more—more than what words and music can convey and an opening to the Not Yet of the Now. This is continued in *HTDAAB* with the closing song "Yahweh":

> Take these hands
> Teach them what to carry
> Take these hands
> Don't make a fist
> Take this mouth
> So quick to criticise
> Take this mouth
> Give it a kiss
>
> Yahweh, Yahweh

Always pain before a child is born
Yahweh, Yahweh
Still I'm waiting for the dawn . . .

For the band that became famous in the late 80s with the agnostic procla-mation "I Still Haven't Found What I'm Looking For," Bono and the band seem to be resting in the assurance that amidst the uncertainty and pain in this life—to paraphrase from *Rattle and Hum*—love has indeed come to town, and for now maybe that is what we need the most.

### Tom Waits—"Jesus Gonna Be Here" and "Day after Tomorrow"

Tom Waits remains one of the unsung heroes of paradoxical theological insights. Take some of these quotes from lyrics from his back catalogue: [lyrics from separate songs separated by blank lines]

The Lord is a very busy man
Jesus is always looking for the big picture.

The bullets that lead straight to the devil's world, just like
marijuana leads to heroine

There ain't no devil, there's just God when he's drunk

Even Jesus wanted just a little more time, when he was walkin'
Spanish down the hall

You can tell me that it's gospel but I know that it's only church

Won't you tell me, brave captain
Why are the wicked so strong
How can the angels get to sleep when the devil leaves his porch
light on?

There's a golden moon that shines up through the mist
And I know that your name can be on that list
There's no eye for an eye there's no tooth for a tooth
I saw Judas Iscariot carrying John Wilkes Booth
He was down there by the train.

If you've lost all hope, if you've lost all your faith
I know you can be cared for, I know you can be safe
And all of the shamefuls, and all of the whores.
And even the soldier who pierced the side of the Lord
Is down there by the train.

While I must admit that I came to Tom Waits late in life, it was certainly in the fullness of time. As Tom sang in "Black Market Baby" (*Mule Variations*, 1999), "There's no prayer like desire," and I certainly desired something more than "safe music" in my early thirties. But I was probably too much of a coward to look beyond my steady diet of singer-songwriters such as Jackson Browne and Bruce Cockburn. As with providence, it's not what we seek that matters so much as what finds us. In the case of Tom Waits, it was as if I had wrestled with an angel and had my hip dislocated in all the right ways. Frankly, I had no idea what was about to hit me. I was over at the home of my then-girlfriend (now wife) when she put *Bone Machine* on the CD player and I heard—no, *experienced*—the opening track. It was "Earth Died Screaming," with all its redemptive horror, like an audio stigmata, or like falling face-first into Flannery O'Connor's *Wise Blood*. While "Earth Died Screaming" is a song for the end of the world— "What does it matter, a dream of love or a dream of lies / We're all going to be in the same place when we die"—"Jesus Gonna Be Here" is a song of sorrowful hope beyond hope amidst a miserable world:

> Well, Jesus gonna be here
> He gonna be here soon, yeah
> He gonna cover us up with leaves
> With a blanket from the moon, yeah
> With a promise and a vow
> And a lullaby for my brow
> Jesus gonna be here
> He gonna be here soon, yeah.

The song has the whiskey-stained tremor of a preacher pushed beyond reason—maybe beyond theology—akin to the psalms of Asaph like Psalm 73. There is sorrow, there is cynicism; but there is also hope, like flowers in the dirt. In the hands of some singer-songwriters, these lyrics would come off as camp, or at worst, painfully unaware of conditions. But somehow Tom Waits can do this, and when I listen to him scratching out a plea for unity and peace, like in "Day after Tomorrow" from his album *Real Gone*, I believe that he is in touch with more humanity than most CCM, Dove Award-winning singer-songwriters I have heard.

> You can't deny, the other side
> Don't want to die anymore than we do
> What I'm trying to say is don't they pray
> to the same god that we do?

And tell me how does god choose
whose prayers does he refuse?
Who turns the wheel
Who throws the dice
on the day after tomorrow
I'm not fighting, for justice
I am not fighting, for freedom
I am fighting, for my life
and another day in the world here.

What I love about the God that Tom Waits muses about and laments for is that his God is earthy in a way that I can touch, taste, feel, and, yes, hear. His world is all too clear to me and very hard to ignore. That seems to be the earthiness of Jesus' ministry, so vivid, so tangible and so painfully attuned to our wavelengths as people who live and breathe and bleed in this world of laughter and pain. That we feel at the deepest parts of what makes us tick is something this guy understands in ways we ourselves don't.

Tom Waits's kingdom of God is filled with one-legged dwarves, blind dogs, drunk preachers, forgotten children, and all humanity in between. The nice thing amidst this "audio *noir*" is that no one is marginalized other than those who find solace in drawing the margins in the first place. In "Sins of the Father," Waits sings a rather insightful charge to the congregation: "God said: don't give me your tin horn prayers." Or perhaps he frames it more pointedly to those who are whining about their middle-class plight in "Come On Up to the House," from *Mule Variations*: "Come down off the cross / we can use the wood." Hope in the Tom Waits universe means that everyone is in it together. This is not about waiting for the end times, it is acknowledging that these are hard times and in order for these hard times to end, we need to be in it together all of the time.

## Fleet Foxes

Fleet Foxes, consisting of Robin Pecknold, Skye Skjelset, Casey Wescott, Christian Wargo, and Josh Tillman, are a Seattle band signed to the labels Sub Pop and Bella Union that has gained international attention in a relatively short period of time. Fleet Foxes released the five-track *Fleet Foxes* EP in 2006, a six-track EP, *Sun Giant*, in the first half of 2008, and their debut full-length self-titled album later that year with Sub Pop. As a debut album, the band quickly accumulated critical and fan praise as their album was given four stars by *Rolling Stone*, and their sound compared to the likes of the Beach Boys, Animal Collective, and Crosby, Stills & Nash. Their self-titled LP received a score of 9.0/10 in *Pitchfork*'s review, which those who follow *Pitchfork* ratings will realize is almost unheard of. Framed by what they term "baroque harmonics," which is a mix of tight multipart vocal harmonies accompanied by tight acoustic instrumentation, their music is at once folk in feel yet closer to rock in punch.

From the liner notes of their debut album, Fleet Foxes make this statement of purpose in regard to their music:

> I can listen to music and instantly be anywhere that song is try-
> ing to take me. Music activates a certain mental freedom in a way
> that nothing else can, and that is so empowering. You can call it
> escapism if you like, but I see it as connecting to a deeper human
> feeling than found in the day-to-day world. . . . Music is a weird
> and cosmic thing, its own strange religion for nonbelievers, and
> what a joy it is to make in any form.

It is this appeal to the sheer beauty of music done for the sake of creating something luminous and transcendent that pushed Fleet Foxes quietly yet resolutely to the forefront of the indie music scene in 2009. Where some bands were seeking to change the world by blasting a hole through it, Fleet Foxes took a page from the Franciscans and stood in the world waiting for the space of silence and then filled it with song. There are not many examples in rock shows (let alone contemporary life) where you can expect to have quiet lifted up and revered. But in a Fleet Foxes show there is something of the Old Lady from Margaret Wise Brown's children's book *Goodnight Moon*, whispering "Hush" over the crowd, and stillness becomes the new rage and revolt in rock and roll. In this way hope is given space to be born for a generation who have banqueted on immediacy, speed of access, and noise. This is something that Fleet Foxes not only encourage in their live shows but demand in order to truly hear what is going on, even in the silence. Many evangelical churches have become afraid of silence, fearing that if we do not fill every space of the senses—filling our ears, our vision, even our touch to the breaking point—that some will not feel engaged and wander away. And yet thousands of fans flock to these Fleet Foxes shows, sitting in stillness as their five-part harmony fills a quiet room. In a review of their debut album, one writer noted that

> Fleet Foxes are able to celebrate what is often lost in the "message" of overtly Christian music—the transcendent quality of music itself. It seems that God has given us something mysterious in music, something that speaks of truth that cannot be spoken, that touches the human heart in ways that words cannot. Fleet Foxes lets the lyrics get out of the way so that the music can be heard.[12]

In a generation that has had every bit of the imagination taken hostage and ransacked by consumerism and the fixation upon the self as the only temple worth worshipping in, Fleet Foxes risk making a space where truth can be found and we can unclench our souls for a time.

Another part of their music that speaks deeply to the sonic mystics that track with the band is that they are truly a *band*. In an article about them in Seattle's *The Stranger* magazine, Megan Seling points out that this is one of the things about them that is so distinctive:

> There is no lead singer in Fleet Foxes. There are guitars, bass, drums, an electric piano, the occasional cello or string of chimes, and many voices. Everyone's voice is an instrument. It's Pecknold you hear most often in songs like "English House" and "Drops in the River," but it's the layers of dense harmonies sung perfectly that make the band's baroque compositions magnificent and vivid. On the song "White Winter Hymnal" specifically, you can't help but think of a bunch of guys sitting around a campfire. The band takes the listener with them out among the trees. While round-robin vocals playfully sing about the river and snow and sun, their big voices reach up to the sky.[13]

As a vehicle of hope, Fleet Foxes' music creates an egalitarian space that encourages people to join in, with no need to wait to be invited. This is the power of the identity of a community over and against the fixation on a leader or figurehead holding all the cards. Hope is something found and forged in the collective in ways that the individualism of the modern age cannot grasp. This is a hope that is strong enough to grow and flourish in silent moments of waiting, not so fragile that we need to create a media flurry in order to crowd all the forces of the world out. If what the Fleet Foxes have hit upon in this new millennium is that "quiet is the new loud," then perhaps the church can listen in as well and learn to wait upon hope once again.

12. Abernathy, "Thoughts On: Fleet Foxes."
13. Seling, "Fleet Foxes Are Not Hippies."

### Leonard Cohen—"The Stranger Song" and "If It Be Your Will"

In an essay, Paul Monk makes this comment about the work of Canadian singer-songwriter Leonard Cohen:

> His unique lyrical style is a wholly contemporary blend of the Psalms and Federico Garcia Lorca, the Chelsea Hotel, Nashville and the Greek islands, Zen Buddhism and the Song of Songs, Franz Rosenzweig and Bob Dylan. Cohen is not an entertainer of spoiled children or politically correct, white-collar workers. He is a master singer of the songs of Zion, by the polluted waters of our post-Christian Babylon. There are few others like him.[14]

Monk goes on to say that if there is a single song that could be called Cohen's signature song it is "The Stranger Song," which was released on his first album, *Songs of Leonard Cohen*, more than forty years ago. It expresses a theme that deeply informs his sense of what human life is about. That theme is the burden of our freedom as something we must forever wrestle with strenuously, against the temptations of "giving up the Holy Game of Poker." Cohen has practiced Zen Buddhism for many years—he worked as a dishwasher at the Zen Center of Mount Baldy outside of LA until the spring of 1999 as the Zen monk "Jikan"—and has been wrestling with this theme of the burden of freedom as an ultimate access to true freedom through "detachment" (what Paul Monk calls his move to becoming a "Zen Cohen" in and of himself).

Although Leonard Cohen has moved "East" in his practice of Zen, his understanding of the burden of freedom is deeply Judaic. Jews have been, from of old, the perennial "strangers" in the world—leaving Ur, leaving Egypt, exiled to Babylon, dispersed across the face of the world, hunted to death by the *goyim*. At several levels of experience and active metaphor, this is at the heart (or heartache) of Cohen's whole body of work: What good is freedom when you are a stranger to everyone? How can someone ever find peace when he or she is destined to be a stranger?

His stranger metaphor runs through his love poetry, his songs of existential fear and despair, and his songs of prophetic darkness. It is for this reason that when his selected poems and songs were published in 1993 he called the book *Stranger Music*. Cohen is certainly one of the most literate of singer-songwriters and has drawn particular insight from the work of Franz Rosenzweig, Martin Buber, and Gershom Scholem.

---

14. Monk, "Under the Spell of Stranger Music."

Rosenzweig's seminal book, *The Star of Redemption*, published in 1921, is probably the ideal theological and philosophical companion to Leonard Cohen's songs. As Cohen sings in "Stranger Song," this life is filled with near encounters and displacement, a sense of discontent, and unrealized intimacy. We are strangers, free but not at home.

> Well, I've been waiting,
> I was sure we'd meet between the trains we're waiting for
> I think it's time to board another
> Please understand,
> I never had a secret chart to get me to the heart of this or any
>     other matter
> When he talks like this you don't know what he's after
> When he speaks like this, you don't know what he's after.
> Let's meet tomorrow if you choose upon the shore,
> beneath the bridge that they are building on some endless river
> Then he leaves the platform for the sleeping car that's warm
> You realize, he's only advertising one more shelter
> And it comes to you, he never was a stranger
> And you say ok the bridge or someplace later.

In an 1993 interview in Britain's *Daily Telegraph*, Cohen said, "I don't consider myself a pessimist at all. I think of a pessimist as someone who is waiting for it to rain. And I feel completely soaked to the skin." There is honesty in someone who has embraced being homeless and out in the rain—the stranger who is free to know that this world is not his home. It is in that life of imperfection and homelessness that Cohen finds solace. As he sings in his song "Anthem" from *The Future* (1992), it is through our imperfection that perfect light can come in: "Ring the bells that still can ring / Forget your perfect offering / There is a crack in everything / It's how the light gets in." We need to continue "ringing the bells that can ring" and embrace that we are ultimately not alone in this life since the Lord of Song sings with us in our displacement and wanderings. The trope of freedom is that it is submission to the Lord of Song where true freedom is born. As Cohen sings in "If It Be Your Will" from *Various Positions* (1985):

> If it be your will that I speak no more
> And my voice be still
> As it was before I will speak no more
> I shall abide until I am spoken for
> If it be your will.

What Leonard Cohen offers us as a corrective is similar to that which Fleet Foxes offer—a willingness to continue on living in the expectation of finding our place of rest, yet also freedom to wander and seek our home in whatever space the Lord of Song should beckon us to. Amidst a generation so fixated on certainty, the faith that Cohen is willing to embrace is truly staggering. Imagine a pastor getting into the pulpit on a Sunday morning and beginning his homily with the words, "As it was before I will speak no more / I shall abide until I am spoken for / if it be you will." There is humility and willingness in Cohen's approach to music that is staggering—a wandering sojourner willing to enter into the wildness of hope that is absent from many big-box churches yet is what the sonic mystics of our land are asking for. Perhaps this is truly a Cohen worth puzzling over.

# 4

# Love

## Living between the Anthem and the Ballad

ONE OF THE TELEVISION shows in recent years that has stirred a revival of appreciation for pop music is *Glee*. Set in a fictional Ohio high school, the show is essentially a mash up of *Le Boheme*, *High School Musical*, *Fame*, *Grease*, *Happy Days*, *Saved by the Bell*, *Flashdance*, and *Bring It On*, set to a K-tel Greatest Hits collection. The story is as old as *Tristen and Isolde* and its Elizabethan redux *Romeo and Juliet*: outcasts driven by a passion for the arts are marginalized by society, and this exclusion fuses a collective that will not only conquer the culture, but will become culture itself. Add to this a never-ending search for meaning and love, and a good dance number and you have the makings of pretty demographically hot TV property. From a monetary standpoint, *Glee* has become the poster child for mass market penetration: rebooting pop songs with new voices (cover songs always work) and virtually tapping into the immediacy of "this new song" by making the song available immediately on iTunes, the show has found a way to sell at multiple angles and thereby ensure a media presence absolutely unparalleled in current television (as I write this three *Glee* collections sit on the list of top ten albums on iTunes). Yet to dismiss the series as merely a money-making scheme conjured up to feed the nostalgia needs of forty-somethings (most of the music trends toward the Gen X era . . . guess someone figured out we still have purchasing power and aren't slackers after all) is to miss a more profound hunger that *Glee* is meeting, albeit in a pop mode, which

85

means that it is never complete and always needing to be recast. It is the hunger for anthems and ballads.

Much of pop music primarily falls into two distinct categories: the *Anthem* and the *Ballad*. Anthems are the rallying cry of 75,000-person stadium concerts, with the audience pumping their fists in the air while standing close enough to the speakers so that the music cuts to the very heart. Such an anthem is usually the lead single for its album and its track listing is often second or third—this is the "Are you with us or against us?" track. This is the "We Will Rock You," "We Are the Champions," "Born in the USA," "We're Not Gonna Take It," "Baba O'Riley," [fill in the blank]. It is the music that grabs us by the shirt and shakes us like a dog tearing into a T-bone steak after not eating for days. This is the soundtrack to the commuter on the highway fist-pumping the roof of his Prius, the iPod jogger speeding up the hill, the base-thumping Honda at the stoplight. Anthems speak about movement, of getting out of here, ending the non-sense job and taking a risk for a change. *In short, Anthems are bigger than we will ever be, and we want to be part of something that big. Ballads, on the other hand, are essentially the song of the heartbreak and remind us just how fragile we really are*: this is the simple Casio-tone keyboard of Yaz's "Only You," the pining piano and synth of Howard Jones's "No One Is to Blame," the Sinéad O'Connor cover of Prince's "Nothing Compares 2U," or Michael Stipe's odes to agnosticism in REM's "Losing My Religion" and "Everybody Hurts."

Somewhere between the anthem and the ballad is where many of us find ourselves—reaching for the confident booming volume and back-beat of the anthem and the painful yet authentic quiet of the ballad. Yet while this is true for millions (see what the top singles are from week to week and the sales figures don't lie) it is not often acknowledged openly. In places of work, in our homes, and in (yes) our churches, life is to be lived in control, measured, under wraps, and it is to be very, very pre-dictable. Basically, while we secretly listen to anthems and ballads in our cars, our iPods, and on our computers, life is lived from one moment of Muzak to another. Devoid of passion, not risking surprises or unbridled emotions, millions feign a life in front of others that is merely a whisper of the anthems and ballads that are the soundtrack of the true, original story. This is why millions of people have turned shows like *Glee* and *High School Musical* into massive hits—they readily admit that we hunger to live in the space of the anthem and the ballad and they turn the dial up to 11 so we can't avoid it.

*What might this have to do with love? Well, just about everything.* In pop music, love is found in the mix of anthems and ballads. Mixtapes and playlists often combine the triumph of the anthem and the fragility of the ballad. Love at its most honest is the clash and embrace of anthems and ballads, not a choice between them nor an attempt to reconcile them. No, love blows the categories apart, reaching to the very depths of our hunger and pain and darkness while fixing our eyes on the brightest star in the heavens. The Gospel accounts of Jesus' life are written as the ultimate mixtape—moments of deep, reflective ballads with a few close friends give way within a few verses to soaring anthemic signs and wonders that draw crowds of five thousand. In this movement between the anthem and the ballad is where love grows and appears in its most full and realized form. The songs below swing between the anthem and the ballad quite readily. Some frame love in sorrow while others move planets with joy unbridled. Yet it is when we play them together that the reality sets in: we will never grow tired of love songs and will always need more to be written.

### Marvin Gaye—"God Is Love"

There is perhaps no better place to begin a discussion of how pop music has brought together the nature of God and the concept of love than with Marvin Gaye. Voted number six in *Rolling Stone*'s list of Greatest Singers of All Time in 2009, Marvin Gaye blends the erotic and deeply spiritual in ways that few ever have, whether in a pop song or a hymn to the Divine. Grammy winner Alicia Keys put it this way in describing the effect Gaye's silky voice had on her and on setting the direction for R & B in the years to come:

> There's no sound like Marvin Gaye: the way he sang so softly, almost gently—but also with so much power. That came straight from the heart. Everything in his life—everything that he thought and felt—affected his singing. The first time I was really introduced to Marvin Gaye was the *What's Going On* album, and I fell in love. It was so moving to hear him talk so desperately about the state of the world, on top of all that brilliant musicality. One of my favorite things he did was to follow the strings with his voice, or double things that the instruments are doing. There's such a simple, subtle lushness to it that adds this whole other layer to the music.

These days we have Pro Tools and a thousand tracks, and you can do different vocals on every track. But back then you really had to innovate, like the way Marvin answered himself in songs, or all that really distant backing work, where his voice is all the way in the back and echoing. It's haunting; he delivered every single song with such clarity that it gave me chills.[1]

Marvin Pentz Gay Junior was born on April 2, 1939. He was one of four children and lived in Washington, DC, with his mother, who worked as a maid and schoolteacher. Gaye's father was the pastor of a small Seventh-Day Adventist congregation called the House of God, which advocated a strict adherence to a blend of Pentecostal fervor and legalism derived from a deeply orthodox reading of the Hebrew Scriptures, for example, Sabbath-keeping practices. His father would later leave the ministry and become involved in Marvin's career, eventually killing his son over a disagreement regarding royalties. As such, Marvin Gaye's music is forever haunted by the church as well as by his longing for a father who would never be there for him as he wished. While songs like "What's Going On" and "I Heard It through the Grapevine" remain his more notable hits, it is two other songs from his 1971 release *What's Going On*—"Wholy Holy" and "God Is Love"—that speak to his desire to see the spiritual and the carnal wrapped into one.

*What's Going On* was a pivotal album for Gaye, taking him into a more mature, politically aware sound that incorporated his renewed spirituality, drawing deeply from his childhood in the church. This was triggered by the sudden death of his close friend Tammi Terrell and represents a significant turning point—one could say this was his life-convicting moment in the sense of James Loder's previously mentioned definition. This album was nothing like the R & B soul with which Gaye had success in the past. He took his music and lyrics to another level, creating an album that, instead of being a series of unrelated songs, is a musical expression, a political comment on the Vietnam War, race relations, spirituality, and what love looks and feels like. What concerns Gaye in "God Is Love" is that the breakdown in society based on politics, race, and lack of belief in anything transcendent is the root of our demise.

This mirrors the concern of the author of 1 John in the New Testament. As the author frames his discussion in this ancient letter with

---

1. Keys, "Marvin Gaye."

the Bible, we see two groups that seem unable to reconcile let alone find common ground. First, there were Jewish Christians, who professed their commitment to Jesus but still felt a loyalty to Judaism. This group would have resembled the Ebonites, a primitive sect of Judaism that had difficulty with the messiahship of Jesus. Secondly, there were Hellenistic Christians, who emerged from a pagan religious background and would have been strongly influenced by the Hellenistic view of salvation, which was dualistic or gnostic in nature. This group would have struggled with the nature of Jesus' full humanity and their view would have resembled Docetism, which is the belief in a Christ of mere spirit without a true body. In John's Gospel, we see that the evangelist's theology is centered on a view of Christ as both one with humanity and one with God. In the letter of 1 John we see a response to these two groups, seeking to draw them together in three distinct ways.

First of all, the letter teaches that to find relationship we must take the focus off of what separates and divides in order to focus upon *a precisely centered reality that is larger than what divides us*—which in the case of 1 John is finding identity in the fullness of Jesus Christ. For those in the community who overextended the humanity of Jesus and diminished his divinity, 1 John asserts that Jesus is preexistent, uncorrupted, and destined for glory in the end (1 John 2:13,14, 20; 3:2, 5, 7). For those who hold to Christ being a divine "phantom" without humanity, 1 John asserts the reality of his life and death on earth (1 John 1:7–9; 2: 6; 4:2, 9, 17). For both sides 1 John presents a Christology that allows tension to exist, with Jesus being at once God and at once human (1:1–4; 2:22–23; 5:1).

Secondly, 1 John provides an *ethic of relationship* that asserts an imperative (3:11, "love one another") with an indicative (4:19, "we love, because he loved us first"). This is a response to some of the Jewish believers, who could have legalistically interpreted the Gospel's love command (John 13:34–35) and not in keeping with the continuity of God's previous acts of grace and mercy. 1 John asserts that this love is not new. Rather, it is new in *an internal, personal* sense as noted in 2:7–8. Conversely, 1 John asserts that this love is *universal* (3:11, 23, 4:7–21) and for all people. This addresses many of the Hellenistic listeners who held a diminished view of Christ's command to love (John 13:34) as only pertaining to their concerns and not to the wider community of the kingdom of God.

This twinned approach at reconciliation found in 1 John is what is at work in Marvin Gaye's "God Is Love." Musically, Gaye generates a choir of voices through call and response, melody and harmony, by taking advantage of his four-octave range and using a multiple tracks to layer his voice—finding the same voice building, separating, and coming together in unity without homogeneity. It is the vocal choir that drives the instrumentation, pushing the bass line and challenging the keyboard to follow as the chorus moves forward:

> He loves us whether or not we know it
> Just loves us, oh ya
> And He'll forgive all our sins
> Forgive all our sins
> And all He asks of us, is we give each other love.
> Oh ya
> Love your mother, she bore you
> Love your father, he works for you
> Love your sister, she's good to you
> Love your brother, your brother
> Don't go and talk about my father, He's good to us,
> God is my friend
> Jesus is my friend.

Teresa L. Reed notes in her book *The Holy Profane: Religion in Black Popular Music* that the tragedies associated with singers like Marvin Gaye "tend to conjure images of the Robert Johnson legend. In exchange for their stardom, some would say, the devil had come to collect his due."[2] Perhaps this is true to some degree. Gaye's life and career ending in murder at the hands of a father he struggled his whole life to love and honor is truly a tragedy. Yet the legacy of challenge that this soul singer left of asking a generation to look beyond its petty differences and to love with the fierce passion of God is a legacy the twenty-first century should look to. For Marvin Gaye, love and passion exist only in relationship—relationship with God and with each other. To attempt to take the spiritual out of the carnal when it comes to love is death, yet so is merely a transcendent idealized love that doesn't have its feet on the ground. To love is to love God and to love neighbor. To truly love is to love both God and neighbor. It is that simple and profound.

---

2. Reed, *Holy Profane*, 96.

### Over the Rhine—"Born"

As a band, Over the Rhine—more specifically, husband-wife duo Karin Bergquist and Linford Detweiler—continues to go deep where others would opt for wider reach or anthemic heights. To call them an "emo" band is simply to miss the mark. They are one of those bands that I enjoy playing when guests are over after the dinner dishes are cleared off the table and waiting for the "Hey . . . who is *this* you put on?" They are people you want to get to know.

From their early releases, such as their classic *Good Dog Bad Dog* and the grand two-disc album *Ohio*, they have been true to their mantra: "Quiet music should be played loud." After touring for *Ohio*, Over the Rhine needed to regroup, not only to reflect on where their art was going, but also to take a look at the state of their marriage.

"A few months into our national tour," wrote Linford on the band's website,

> Karin and I realized that although good things were happening with our music, there was just very little energy or creativity or time left over for our marriage, and it was taking a toll on us. I think we had to learn that putting a long-term relationship on autopilot indefinitely can be dangerous if not fatal. We decided we had to pull the plug on the tour and go home and figure out if being together was something we were still committed to.
>
> We opted to start over, reinvent our own relationship, dig deep and do the homework to see if we could make our marriage sing. We decided to redirect the same thought and energy that we had been putting into writing and performing, toward our life at home together. We prayed a lot. Our friends prayed a lot. It was the beginning of a wonderful new chapter for us. And hopefully, some of what we've learned has not only made us better people, but better songwriters as well.[3]

The result of their labors was the 2005 release *Drunkard's Prayer*, one of their best recordings to date. It was recorded in their living room and reflects the relaxed atmosphere and sonic warmth that can only be found at home when one discovers, like Alice after she falls down the rabbit hole, that we always could have gone home if we had wanted to. There is a consistent vibe of fragility and desire throughout each track, as if you've just filled a wine glass and set it before someone you have longed to talk

---

3. Detweiler, "Drunkard's Prayer: Notes."

to, only to discover you've lost the words along the way. Perhaps this is not merely a metaphor, given what Linford said about the song "Born": "When we came home from the tour, we bought two cases of wine and decided we were going to put a bottle on the kitchen table every evening and start talking until nothing was left. The idea was not to get drunk, but to talk face to face deep into the night."[4] As Karin sings in "Born," part of this discovery over the stilled glass of wine and the hope for connection is found in learning to "love without fear":

> Secret fears, the supernatural
> Thank God for this new laughter
> Thank God the joke's on me
>
> We've seen the landfill rainbow
> We've seen the junkyard of love
> Baby it's no place for you and me
>
> I was born to laugh
> I learned to laugh through my tears
> I was born to love
> I'm gonna learn to love without fear.

Anyone who has loved, lost love, and longed to love knows how wrapped up love is with fear. This is not new, nor is it foreign to the witness of the prophet Isaiah through to the annunciation of the angel Gabriel to young Mary: God has been saying "fear not" for quite a long time, along with "love one another." It seems to be a package deal. Yet in the small, quiet space of a marriage, this portrait of radical hope poured out in reckless love is one that is subsequently spilled out into Over the Rhine's songs, and we are the better for it. With upright bass, piano, acoustic guitars, a few horns, a few subtle textures, and Karin's sublime voice, "Drunkard's Prayer" is served, like a glass of fine Pinot Noir, as a toast to risking love in the face of fear, something that you settle into at twilight and find that fragile longing and silent anticipation can come home with us, especially when love opens the door.

### Death Cab for Cutie—"Title and Registration"

Ben Gibbard, lead singer and songwriter for Death Cab for Cutie and The Postal Service, quickly became a leading voice—literally and figuratively—for indie pop in the early twenty-first century. While the likes of Coldplay

---

4. Ibid.

and Radiohead continue to fill arenas, for Death Cab this sense of immediacy and intimacy found in big arena bands is built on the false assumption that stadium-sized success implies authenticity. Granted, their respective paranoias—Coldplay's Chris Martin's discontent with relationships and Radiohead's Thom Yorke's Luddite-like fear that technology will eclipse the human spirit—ring true with many folks. But Ben Gibbard is following a different path both sonically and spirituality. *He seems to believe that the world is somehow a fundamentally happy place.* Take "The New Year," the opening track from Death Cab's breakthrough album *Transatlanticism*. While the lyrics describe a level of discontent and an ill-at-ease feeling with the advent of a new beginning ("So this is the New Year / and I don't feel any different"), it is the hope of something more and the possibility of connection that ends the song amidst glacial open-chord guitar riffs that build toward conclusion rather than dissonance:

> I wish the world was flat like the old days
> Then I could travel just by folding a map
> No more airplanes or speed trains or freeways
> There'd be no distance that can hold us back.

Like his sonic forefather Art Garfunkel, Ben Gibbard's voice has a gentle, childlike quality that offers a simple, uncluttered purity. It's like the wonder we might experience when hearing the opening strains of the young soloist in Handel's "Comfort Ye My People" from *The Messiah* in a half-lit room. As cynical as we may be, the simple purity of the voice draws us into a hope often too painful to admit in our tempest-tossed world. Sometimes, in addition to well-turned words in a lyrically rich song or sonically sublime orchestration, we need voices like Ben Gibbard's—voices able to convey wonder and contentment, voices without regret, voices infused with a willingness to laugh in ways we somehow sacrificed when we left Eden.

In the track "Title and Registration", Gibbard's voice signals the importance that artifacts play in how we hold onto the resonance of love through physical objects that help us locate our deep spiritual longings. The protagonist in the song launches into an existential reflection on what would seem the most mundane of song topics—a car glove compartment. This space in the car that we dump everything from old city maps to automobile pink slips to hairbrushes is something that is "inaccurately named" given that it rarely has anything to "keep our fingers warm" let alone our very being. While fumbling for his car's title and registration, artifacts of past love fall out unexpected and unannounced—photographs long forgotten of past love now lost. As Gibbard laments in this reflection while watching his lover's headlights drive away into the east, finding these "souvenirs from better times" when he was looking for something else means that love is never truly lost and can come back in a flash. As discussed in the introduction of the book in regard to the power of pop music to draw us into places where we no longer have control, Gibbard's desire to re-label the glove compartment is to acknowledge that mundane things like old photos and old pop songs can (and often do) spring out unannounced and perhaps we need warning labels to caution people. Much like parent advisory labels have been placed on everything from Hip Hop CDs to websites, Gibbard is acknowledging that our memories are perhaps the more dangerous thing of all. Love as Gibbard reminds us is not always something we find or seek after, but often something that will find us in the space where "disappointment and regret collide." Bittersweet though it may be, pop music can teach us that sometimes it is the love that we have lost that reminds us what love is about after all.

### Coldplay—*X&Y*

As I have previously mentioned, during the six years I lived in Scotland, I had the privilege of seeing some great shows in Glasgow at a wee club of great renown called King Tut's Wah Wah Hut. Like The Cave in Liverpool, King Tut's has launched numerous bands into stardom, including Oasis, Del Amtri, and Belle and Sebastian, and it even played a role in the humble beginnings of what some call the next "U2"—Coldplay.

In 2000, Chris Martin and his merry band toured like maniacs throughout the UK, stopping at King Tut's for a crazy show of covers and a pair of strong singles. One of the singles was "Shiver," with its Radiohead-riffing fits and starts, belying a calm, confident grace; the other was "Yellow," the single that put them on the map. What continues to distinguish Coldplay from other neo-British rockers is a fresh sound amidst a sea of Oasis and Radiohead wannabes. (Pick up Travis, Stereophonics, Idlewild, and Embrace and tell me what's distinctive.)

Coldplay's debut album, *Parachutes*, became a critical and commercial hit in 2000 and was followed in 2002 by their sophomore bestseller, *A Rush of Blood to the Head*. The album featured some great singles with super hooks, like "The Scientist," "Clocks," and "In My Place," songs that dig into the sing-along portion of your mind. Most of the production questionables from *Parachutes* seem to have been ironed out in *Rush of Blood*; there were enough smooth edges and open spaces to confirm Coldplay's quantum leap from young, moody rockers (signified by itchy guitar) to mature, moody rockers (signified by piano). The conditions of their prior melancholy had presumably changed, but the song remained the same. Rather than sounding like a guitar band, they were beginning to sound like a Chris Martin band, and that is not a bad thing.

With the release of *X&Y* in 2005, the devolution looked complete. As the band grew more comfortable with their billing as proper stars—"the next U2" was the most common tag—they grow more reliant on Martin, the only member with proper star qualities. And *X&Y* is a record that defers, tragically, to the singer. Many of the songs open with a spotlighted Martin unfurling his lyrical sadness before the band even has a chance to get into a rhythm, play a note, or even unpack their equipment. There are cavernous, wide-open spaces carved out of the songs so that Martin's loud-soft-loud cries can evoke maximum drama. As Hua Hsu's review in *Slate* put it,

> There are epic tissue-boxes of emotion, but no objective correlative to account for the tears. Most of the album treads in the lost-in-love territory of trite tunes like "Fix You" or "The Hardest Part." "What If" borrows a device from the pop philosophizing of John Lennon's "Imagine," only it descends from depressing questions of space and time and Manichean divides to the more pressing issue: "What if you should decide / That you don't want me there by your side?" There is nothing wrong with performing emotion in song— this is what pop music does. But there is something suspicious about overdramatizing the terms of those emotions.[5]

I couldn't agree more with Hsu's summation. The overwrought haranguing on the album can't possibly carry Chris Martin's lyrics about a flawed lover in need of fixing. This is the classic problem with bands that seek after our hearts through trials and empathy. How much empathy can a huge rock band possibly have with little old me? How much less so when the lead singer is married to Gwyneth Paltrow! In short, *X&Y* has some of the feelings right and even some of the vibe, but the questions that bring us to the point of loss, loneliness, and despair seem a million miles away. Is this what rock does to us? Does it offer us the *cura animarum* but leave us to figure out the sickness on our own?

5. Hsu, "Melancholy Arena Rock: Why Is Coldplay Still Depressed?"

But in the stillness of small spaces, the music of bands like Coldplay works listeners over. There is a reason millions of copies of Coldplay CDs and digital downloads will be played through earbuds in MP3 players and small dashboard speakers. The magic of bands like Coldplay, U2, Dave Matthews Band and other arena-sized acts that can both fill 60,000-seat stadiums and find comfort in our car stereos on rainy nights is that the call for intimacy in their ballads are large emotions deep within us yet so private that we only whisper along with the lyrics in the anonymity of a large gathering or the isolation of our earbuds.

One grand example of how arena rock works better in small spaces is found in the title track "X & Y." As Chris Martin begins the song, he admits that what he is trying to put to words—how is it that we find intimacy and love between a man (X) and a women (Y) when we are broken people—is beyond his control and ability to describe let alone bring together:

> Trying hard to speak and
> Fighting with my weak hand
> Driven to distraction
> So part of the plan
> When something is broken
> And you try to fix it
> Trying to repair it
> Any way you can

No matter huge large the sound, no matter how massive the stadium, no matter how famous the band or its celebrity front man, the struggle to describe the rise and fall of love is always difficult. As the song and album title clearly show, the space between people—shown with the ampersand symbol "&"—divides us and yet love continues to challenge us to overcome this divide and find the intimacy that we long for. Knowing that he can't overcome the divide and heal the brokenness, Martin takes a rather bold move for someone used to filling stadiums—he confesses his failure in a whisper that requires us to listen closely rather than lean back as a member of the audience. It is this confession coupled with testimony—"I wanna love you/But I don't know if I can/I know something is broken/And I'm trying to fix it/Trying to repair it/ Any way I can"—that redeems Coldplay's attempts to speak for everyone at the margins while they sit in the throne of stardom and why a large arena isn't where we find the complete truth of love. True, we gather in these audiences of 'fan faith' along with thousands of other sonic mystics seeking to connect to one another and hopefully to the transcendent behind all the words and music, but when we put on the headphones and hear the impossibility of love from someone who has everything the culture desires—money, fame, glory, beauty—we understand that love is bigger than all of us and find courage to sing along in hopes that love can be healed and love's labor will not be in vain after all.

### Elton John—"Tiny Dancer"

Is the deepest notion of love the discovery that something other than yourself is worth loving? Perhaps part of adulthood is coming to grips with this truth, but I certainly didn't fully understand it as a teenager although I glimpsed at it through pop music. To say that the 1970s were kind to me would be a lie. Granted, I am still here to tell the tale and that counts for something, but the 70s represented a period of unbelievable angst. I was the shortest kid in my class through ninth grade (that's me in the class picture in the front row holding the class sign). Add that to the fact that I had clinical acne, which I treated with a roll-on solution that made me look like a lumpy case of jaundice, and you have quite a package. My struggle to figure out what I was looking for in life rarely extended beyond not getting thrown into a locker by some older kid with an AC/DC shirt. I am in my "top 40s" now, so I suppose I should be thankful that I have the distance I do from such events, but given that the 70s continue to be reimagined, I think it's time to set the record straight.

True enough, the 1970s may be remembered in current *Zeitgeist* as the time of white slacks, Jimmy Carter, and music adhering to the ABC's (ABBA, the Bee Gees, and Cat Stevens to name a few) of adult-oriented radio (AOR). This was the period that saw the Stones' *Sticky Fingers*, Led Zeppelin's *Fourth* album, and big records from T. Rex and Rod Stewart hitting the airwaves with force. But when I was living through the 70s, it wasn't force that I needed most, it was empathy. As I tried to embrace Robert Plant in seventh grade, it was Elton John's subtle sound, coupled with Bernie Taupin's catchy lyrics, that continued to capture the broadest audience and to speak of loneliness in ways I remember needing to hear. Among Elton John's early albums, two continue to stand out: *Honky Chateau*, a masterpiece that included "Mona Lisas and Madhatters," "Rocket Man," and "Madman across the Water." The latter is named for a cut that originally appeared on his album *Tumbleweed Connection* and yielded some of his earliest AOR staples. "Tiny Dancer," like the previous

"Your Song," was introduced and carried by John's masterful piano composition. The song's sense of longing also employed the falsetto chorus that would become as much of a trademark as his costumes. "Levon," another entry into the John-Taupin "ballad of" category, is one of their finest pieces. Interestingly, there are references to "God," "Lord," or "Jesus" on six tracks on this collection. I wouldn't say any of these six songs has a religious theme, but it is interesting how Taupin folded in these references on this album.

"Tiny Dancer" is an ode to Bernie Taupin's wife and celebrates the Elton John Band's highly successful first trip to the USA in 1970, after which rapturous popular and critical acclaim soon saw John become the pop chart star of the decade. It is about the power of music and the joy of being a fan. The magic of the song is a celebration of being "in the zone"—that moment we all find ourselves in when for four minutes we are "in" a pop song. Time stands still, yet it soars, and everything becomes possible. For me, "Tiny Dancer" is about getting up the courage to ask a girl to dance with me at the Jane Addams Junior High fall dance. The attempt was a failure—"You wanna dance?" "Ahh . . . no"—but every time I hear the song, I feel some of that courage come back nonetheless. This is captured brilliantly in Cameron Crowe's 2000 movie *Almost Famous*, which is his ode to the 1970s. In a great scene where Stillwater's lead guitarist and iconic figure Russell Hammond (played by Billy Crudrup) has had a falling-out with the band and is sitting in painful silence on the tour bus, "Tiny Dancer" starts to play. Slowly, each member of the band begins to join in, singing along with the tune, with grins spreading across every face. There is a sense of euphoria as the volume rises in the bus, enfolding members of a family that had become so lost in their own agendas and ego that they had forgotten, literally, the joy of the songs that they sang together. In that moment of release and restoration, they belt out the lyrics: "Jesus Freaks out in the streets / handing out tickets for God / Turning back, she just laughs / The boulevard is not that bad." I remember looking around the dark movie theater at that moment and seeing people silently mouthing the words to "Tiny Dancer" along with the joyous reunion of Stillwater on the flickering screen. The *benedictus* of the scene comes when Patrick Fugit's William Miller whispers to Kate Hudson's Penny Lane, "I need to go home." As the audience and Stillwater continue to sing along with Elton's chorus—"Hold me closer, tiny dancer . . ."—Penny Lane's reply cuts to the quick: "You are home."

Elton John has had his moments both great and downright scary in the past few decades since "Madman on the Water" and "Tiny Dancer." But he continues to invite the lonely and lost to a place of home amidst the common heartbreaks of life like few pop musicians have ever done. As many churches continue to draw its fellowship into selfish praise music filled with painful first-person self-importance, I am thankful for moments when I can sing along with those seeking hope framed in a selfless love, along with that pimpled teenager that I was and the adult I am growing into, as well as with others seeking to "hand out tickets for God" as we all "count the headlights on the highway," each of us asking the very same questions but at least not doing it alone.

### Snow Patrol—"Run"

One of the things that makes love—whether romantic, familial, communal, or spiritual—so profound is not merely the moment of being in love, but being with the people you discover are worth loving and should be loved with the fierceness of what fires the stars and moves the ocean. It is also the way in which our memories continue to frame a portrait and sustain our love for those around us even when we or they are away. There is a long tradition in popular music of writing about what happens when that last encore is sung, the house lights go up, and the audience fights their way toward the parking lot to the sound of the mixtape the roadies put together. It seems to hit artists after their first big tour, this need to express the experience of being the rock stars they had dreamed of and the raw emotion of finding out that after the bright lights and big noise, they still need to connect and find intimacy. There is a subgenre of these songs about the look and feel of being before the roaring crowds of the stadium (Journey's "Faithfully," for example, with its reference to "circus lights"), the feeling of emptiness when the crowd has gone and the performer is left alone on the stage (Jackson Browne's album of the road, *Running on Empty*, with the classic post-concert tune "The Loadout"), or just the longing for connection that is hinted at but not consummated when a performer feels the crush of the monitor around his ankles and the burn of the light gels above the stage and sees the mixing hues of the audience's faces in an emo-wash montage like a Caspar David Friedrich or the post-punk pointillism found in a Georges-Pierre Seurat. Another entry into this subgenre is Snow Patrol's great single "Run" from their third album, *Final Straw*.

Reviewers have raved about Snow Patrol for a while now. The trio from Dundee, Scotland, have far-ranging influences and paint with both big brushes and pinpoint accuracy. According to lead singer Gary Lightbody, "Basically our favorite bands were poured into [*Final Straw*] and at the time we were under the influence of American rock—the Pixies, Dinosaur Jr, Soundgarden—but we were listening to My Bloody Valentine and the first Super Furry Animals album too."[6]

"Run" is a song of departure and hope for a real tomorrow long after the buzz in your ears and the after-concert blur comes into real-time focus. As the song opens, the singer is playing his last encore for a fan:

> I'll sing it one last time for you
> Then we really have to go
> You've been the only thing that's right
> In all I've done.

As the singer and the fan blend into the music, the euphoria of being "in" the song becomes the *via media* between losing the self and beginning the afterlife:

> Louder louder
> And we'll run for our lives
> I can hardly speak I understand
> Why you can't raise your voice to say.

Theology talks quite a bit about "performativity," the notion that what we believe is only as real as what we do. Songs like "Run" turn the mirror back on the performer as well as the audience and ask a question: After the lights come back on and the amps are unplugged, what then? Are we lost in the longing to return to that moment when the "louder, louder" cry bleeds out all the thoughts of our oh-so-mundane lives? Are we hoping that the fantasy constructed in the eyes of the adoring fan may actually be love in all its height, its depth, its breadth? For Christians caught up in the "shock and awe" of blasting guitars, Casio-lite keyboards, and clanging drums while a row of "worship leaders" rhyme "dove" with "love from above," is the desire for "louder, louder" really a cry to retreat into the moment of noise or to take hold of the *benedictus* of sending into a risky life in the flesh? In many ways the end of the encore in any live show is a moment when we stand together—audience and artist—after having gone

---

6. Zimmerman, "Snow Patrol."

through the momentary loss, the return of the artist for another round of songs, and then finally that moment when we all say goodbye. In this moment the audience is given a task as the lights come up and shuffle off to our cars: Will we remember not only the music, the artist, and the crush of the crowds, but also hold the memory open as a space of possibility for others to be invited into? As we share with others the amazing experience of the concert, there is a vulnerability in even the slightest glimmer in our eyes that what we are sharing in this memory is something we are passionate about, something that has formed us, and that we would love to go and be a part of again and again. The stewarding of memories is how love is kept alive and kindled into a flame of possibility for others. "Wow . . . that sounds amazing. Can I borrow that CD?" Love is contagious like that, even in the aftermath and memories long since past. "Run" is just one example of the artist knowing this as well, and a reminder for those of us who find ourselves on stages or in the parking lot after the song is fading in our ears that it is still alive in our hearts and its meaning is still worth exploring, because love can come alive long after the moment it starts is gone.

### Beck—"Everybody's Got to Learn Sometime," from *Eternal Sunshine of the Spotless Mind* Soundtrack

One of the most important areas of music in recent years is the interplay of music and film in that wonderful aspect of the post-Vietnam-era shift in cinema: the soundtrack. Movies have always looked to music to give their images depth, pathos, and at certain moments something of the divine. This is often found in the musical score, an instrumental piece written to elicit the emotive overture of the filmic narrative. In contrast to the score, soundtracks draw from individual artists who provide iconic moments—short, dense tableaus that act as a musical counterpoint and compliment to the film's storyline. It was the megablast of the soundtrack to *Saturday Night Fever* in 1977 that made soundtracks not merely emotional signposts for narrative but a financial boon for the industry. Most soundtracks are pretty forgettable and downright awful. But occasionally, an artist embraces the directorial vision of a film and creates something so subtle and sublime that to hear the song not only transports us back to the visual narrative but links our lives to the pathos and the joy in a wondrous way.

As a medium we merely "view," film becomes something we often understand without struggling to improve our understanding. For example, the photographic image stands in contrast to a text, which, with a single word, can shift from representation to reflection. We look at a photo and recall its source; its very stillness seems to encourage us to make a reference, like "Who is in the picture?" or "When was it taken?" or "Where was that building in the background?" It is this which led cultural theorist Roland Barthes to call the photographic image pure contingency—that is, the photograph is always something that is representational and therefore contingent on something other for meaning to arise. In contrast, and more so than for other arts, film offers *an immediate and fully contextualized presence to the world.* It is self-referential and makes its own reality. Ironically, as James Monaco notes, it is precisely because films "so very clearly mimic reality that we apprehend them much more easily than we comprehend them." Add music to the mix and you have a full experience that allows the viewer-listener to apprehend a moment of meaning with all of the senses engaged—meaning without mediation. No wonder we love the movies.

One new writer-director on the scene who uses music to whisper rather than to shout the core message of his films is Charlie Kaufman, writer of such films as *Being John Malkovitch, Adaptation,* and *Eternal Sunshine of the Spotless Mind.* "I like to live in the confusion," says the writer of his preference for chaos over the concrete. "When you complicate things, that's when things are more interesting."[7] Always an avid reader, though loath to list influences lest his work be compared to theirs, Kaufman has read authors ranging from Franz Kafka, Samuel Beckett, Stanislaw Lem, Philip K. Dick, and Stephen Dixon to Shirley Jackson and Patricia Highsmith, who both specialize in "the queasy, really subtle sh*t that happens between characters; it can seem like nothing's happening, but it's horrible just the same."[8] One of the things I love about Charlie Kaufman is his attempt to model his scripts and film projects on the work of Flannery O'Connor, who believed that Southern writers aptly render "the grotesque" because they can still recognize what it is. Reading O'Connor made Kaufman fear "that I wouldn't have a voice because I didn't seem to come from anywhere—I was jealous of other parts of America." Part of Kaufman's own development came from recognizing the "weirdness" within his purview. Some of his favorite films include *What Happened Was . . .* (Tom Noonan), *Naked* (Mike

7. BeingCharlieKaufman.com, "Biography."

8. Sragow, "Being Charlie Kaufman."

Leigh) , *Safe* (Todd Haynes), *Ladybird Ladybird* (Ken Loach), *Eraserhead* (David Lynch) and "most of the Coen brothers and David Lynch things."[9]

It makes sense that someone as *non-sequitur* as Charlie Kaufman would find the ideal soundtrack partner in Beck. One of the most inventive and eclectic figures to emerge from the 90s alternative revolution, Beck is the epitome of postmodern chic in an era obsessed with junk culture. Drawing upon a kaleidoscope of influences—pop, folk, psychedelia, hip-hop, country, blues, R & B, funk, indie rock, noise rock, experimental rock, jazz, lounge, Brazilian music—Beck has created a body of work that is wildly unpredictable, vibrantly messy, and bursting with ideas. He is unquestionably a product of the media age—what market-driven folks call "Generation M" for *media*—and a true "recombinantist" whose concoctions are pasted together from bits of the past and the present in ways that could only occur to an overexposed pop-culture junkie. Beck may seem like a chaotic artist, with his "Loser" and "Where It's At" being extreme mash-ups of random sources, but his signature musical voice is forged in characters in this post-essentialist age that are rootless and sprawling in diversity and find self-determination through the acknowledgement that the self has no boundaries or conventions due to its *imago Dei*-forged depth.

One song that seems to capture the simplicity of Beck's music is "Everybody's Got to Learn Sometime," which frames the musical signature of Kaufman's *Eternal Sunshine of the Spotless Mind*. "Change your heart / Look around you . . . change your heart / It will astound you . . . I need your lovin' / like I need the sunshine / Everybody's got to learn sometime . . ." is the lyric that repeats throughout the images that flash on the screen. As a movie that plays with the notion of how identity is formed through memory—can we love if we can't remember who or whose we are?—the simplicity of the repeated lyric is contemplative and sacramental, drawing the viewer of the film to "remember" the line. To repeat it is to bring it into truth. The repeated simplicity of the track coupled with the non-linear nature of Kaufman's (literal) stream-of-consciousness narrative brings a wonderful reminder, as Tolkien stated so well, that not all those who wander are lost.

### Gary DeCarlo—"Kiss Him Goodbye"

Is it me or do songs that degenerate into post-linguistic revelry provoke the uncontrollable drive to sing along? I have found this utterly ironic.

9. BeingCharlieKaufman.com, "Biography."

Once language moves beyond the framing of a linguistic system and into the pure utterance of sound *qua* sound—like "la la la"—we feel we want to join in and that we have been invited to do so. For example, think of the 1969 song "Kiss Him Goodbye," written by Gary DeCarlo, Dale Frashuer, and Paul Leka. Surely this is one of the most covered songs in pop music given its popularity at sporting events as a trumpet blast to the competition from the soon-to-be-winning fans that the game is about up.

The lyrics as written are a mess. Here is the chorus:

> Na na na na, na na na na, hey hey hey, goodbye [repeat many times and fade out].

But who *cares* about the messiness? Even the staunchest, dourest, most stoic churchman will open his wee gob and belt this out alongside the roaring masses. This is the same man who in a different environment will sit stock-still through a song with lyrics drawn straight from the Psalter, in silent protest against the choice of instrumentation.

We see the same simple-lyric, sing-along phenomenon in "The Night They Drove Ol' Dixie Down" by The Band:

> The night they drove Old Dixie down
> And the bells were ringing
> The night they drove Old Dixie down
> And the people were singin'
> They went la la la la la la la la la la la la la.

I could cite many more examples.

Part of what drives this home for me is that this is where my daughters join in as well, as happened once when we were singing along to Ernie and Bert's *Sesame Street* classic, "The La La La Song," in which Ernie and Bert try to think of words that begin with *L* ( "La la la laughter. . . . La la la lumps in my oatmeal . . ."). The girls love this song, and they belted out their respective choices throughout the three-minute ditty. "This is such a fun song, Daddy," my oldest once told me. "I like songs that smile." Pop songs "that smile" speak to us in ways we can't explain, and often neither can the artists who wrote them. Not able to find words for our feelings of joy or sorrow, music can still find expression through a series of "la la las" or "oh oh ohs," which in writing make no sense but in music—as with life—make all the sense in the world. Love is like that isn't it?—pushing us beyond the placeholders of language systems and into places where we have no language but still have heart.

I am not advocating for barking and howling through a worship service by any means—that is, unless the Spirit moves you in that direction. But sometimes worship should provide the most guttural points of entry for anyone wishing to enter in. Yes, maybe even language itself moves aside to bid welcome and invite those who can make some noise—any at all—to the congregational gathering of song. Sometimes I think of this at Christmas when churches decide not to sing "Silent Night" but only hum it together in the silent darkness broken by the flickering of candle flame. It still moves me to hear the humming, maybe because there is something there that I can't put my finger on, something I can't quite comprehend, beating deep below my understanding. Maybe we just need to hum along a bit more in church or offer some freedom for "la la la" every once and a while so that what is hidden behind well-framed words can come out in new ways.

### John Doe (with Jane Wiedlin)—"Forever with You"

I need to say one thing at the outset: I was never cool enough for punk.

As a theologian in my forties, I doubt my street cred in punk circles could ever be established, so I won't even try. Granted, I love The Clash and living in the UK gave me a deeper appreciation for "The Guns of Brixton" as art and much-needed social commentary. What I appreciate the most about punk is the constant move against being categorized. To be labeled "punk" *per se* is to be labeled *not punk*. The church often errs in the search for categories and labels, which end up being the source of praise and argumentation instead of illuminating the content toward which the labels and categories are supposed to point. As we saw in the move at times away from language systems and into "la la las" and "oh oh ohs," punk also pushes hard against easily categorized statements and tries to awaken the listener and world around to something beyond words.

Perhaps this is why, in the punk family, John Doe and X make sense to me. They're a band and a band member that are essentially *non-labeled*. The Los Angeles band X was formed in 1977 after songwriter and bassist John Doe met Exene Cervenka, whom he would later marry and divorce, at a Venice poetry workshop. With rockabilly veteran Billy Zoom on guitar and DJ Bonebrake on drums, the band garnered an immediate following and attracted the attention of former Doors keyboardist Ray Manzarek, who took the new band into the studio for *Los Angeles* in 1980. In theory, punkers and folkies didn't find a lot in common to talk about, especially in in the late 70s, when both camps were fighting a common enemy—disco. Nevertheless, not only was X's merging with an ex-Doors member tolerated, it earned them stature as California's preeminent punk band when *Los Angeles* received across-the-board rave reviews.

1981 saw the release of the similarly punked-up *Wild Gift*, while X's 1982 album *Under the Big Black Sun* began what would be a long career in merging hard rock, country, and folk into their fiery mix. The band successfully began to mix in their populist politics with an eye toward matters of the heart.

Lead singer and songwriter John Doe was dreamed up in Los Angeles in January or February 1977 after an exhausting trip from Baltimore on the previous Halloween. As Doe says in his bio, speaking in the third person about his persona:

> [John Doe eventually] settles in Venice, CA ('cause that's where the Beats lived), goes to the Venice poetry workshop and meets Exene. X band starts, records a single, gets more popular (1979 there was a line around the block at the Whisky), signs to Slash Records and by 1981 the L.A. "punk-rock explosion" is all but over. X's first two records have poetry and hard rock; it connects with the audience's guts and brains and the critics really like it.[10]

John Doe's solo album, *Forever Hasn't Happened Yet*, is often on constant iPod rotation during my commute. Where most people see punk rockers as screamers without a voice, John Doe has an authentic sound with tons to say. While this comparison will seem praise to some and blasphemy to others, John Doe treads much the same path as Bruce Springsteen and gets equally striking results. Punk is like folk music in its need to tell stories of truth. The difference in genre is that while folk will walk slowly through metaphor, punk is existentially Marxist in its direct, no-holds-barred, in-your-face approach. In this way, *Forever Hasn't Happened Yet* plays the *via media*, blending cracking punk and introspective folk with a casual intensity. What is stunning about the record is just how easygoing this effort seems. Doe just gives the impression that making razor-sharp music with keen insight is oh-so-easy. "Twin Brother," Doe's heartbreaking duet with Grant-Lee Phillips, is about as good as this kind of music can get and reminds me of what people seemed to mean by *Americana* before it got corporate. There are hints of the Lizard King Jim Morrison on "The Losing Kind," and "Hwy. 5," a great duet with Neko Case that

10. Doe, "John Doe: Biography."

John Doe wrote with his by-then ex-wife Exene Cervenka, recalls his old band's later years. It has all the funk and swagger that made punk in the 70s something more than noise. It was the heartache of beat poets, amped up and storming the stage with truth in its teeth.

In many ways, given the tragedies in America's Southland after Hurricane Katrina, Doe's lyrics seem poignant. In the end, after religious, governmental, and institutional systems have faded away amidst tragedy, we are left with each other. Perhaps this is where we begin to understand what forever will look like as we finally see one another in the aftermath, shame, and grace that comes.

> We're not united
> But stand for each other
> When the whole world let us down
> No red, white, and blue
> No more 'underground'
> Standing up for you
> I'm forever for you . . .

If this is what it means to be punk, maybe John Knox was more like Sid Vicious than I thought.

### Madonna—"Live to Tell"

Some rather significant things happened in pop music during the 80s that continue to shape culture at large, many of which are one-named wonders: Sting, Cher, Prince, the ubiquitous Bono, and of course, Madonna.

Arguably one of the most instrumental forces in music and pop culture, Madonna continues to amaze and astound critics by recreating herself time and again just when she seems to have hit the wall. Her recent interest in some Hollywood form of Kabala notwithstanding, Madonna's music has always carried a deeper understanding of spirituality than most people would be willing to credit her with. Take her 1986 album *True Blue*, for example. Released during my last year in college, during a time when George H. W. Bush was ascending to the Oval Office, Demi Moore was in *St. Elmo's Fire*, and the first Iraq crisis was introducing us to Saddam Hussein, *True Blue* was a mammoth worldwide success. CD purchases were eclipsing LP sales, but you could still see Madonna's platinum-blonde head thrown back in ecstasy on big album covers through the windows of Tower Records stores. *True Blue* reached number one in the US and twenty-seven other countries—an unprecedented success at the time for a female artist—and spawned five smash singles. The leadoff track, "Live to Tell," hit number one in the US and was followed by four more top-five tracks: "Papa Don't Preach" (no. 1), "True Blue" (no. 3), "Open Your Heart" (no. 1) and "La Isla Bonita" (no. 4). The album cemented her chart domination in the UK, where "Papa Don't Preach," "True Blue," and "La Isla Bonita" all hit number one. Showing herself to be a multimedia star bar none, she not only wrote and produced the album but was also the artistic director for all the music videos for the singles. "Papa Don't Preach" scored a nod for the Female Pop Vocal Performance Grammy award. *True Blue* is certainly one of Madonna's bestselling studio albums worldwide, with estimated sales at twenty million.

My memories of the single "Live to Tell" will always be wrapped up, like most memories of music in the 80s, with its accompanying music video. James Foley directed the video for the song, which was also included on the soundtrack to Foley's film *At Close Range*. Foley later went on to direct Madonna in her first major movie outing, *Who's That Girl?*, as well as her "Papa Don't Preach" video, some episodes of *Twin Peaks*, and the David Mamet masterpiece *Glengarry Glen Ross*. The fact that "Live to Tell" is a ballad makes it a strange song for a lead single, but it continues to be a haunting memory and, I would argue, one of the best things Madonna has ever done. It is a simple song set within a very simple video. The camera pulls into a darkened room where one spotlight is on the platinum head of Madonna, whose back is turned to the camera. As she slowly turns to face the camera, she looks directly through the lens at the viewer—no leaping over boy toys in S&M gear as in her later *Erotica*-era videos—and we see the empty longing in her expression as the camera maintains its fixation on her. As the music moves forward and the various flashes of clips from *At Close Range* jump cut in and out of the video, we still find Madonna alone, in a darkened room, in a basic Laura Ingalls Wilder-esque prairie dress. There is something in that loneliness that makes it feel like the most authentic thing Madonna has ever done. The effect is similar to watching Carl Theoder Dreyer's 1928 masterpiece *La Passion de Jeanne d'Arc*, or Sinéad O'Connor's video for her 1990 cover of "Nothing Compares 2 U"— open and vulnerable to the point of being painful because that level of vulnerability calls us out in ways we strongly desire but can't reciprocate.

"Live to Tell" is a typical pop song. At about four minutes and thirty seconds, it doesn't overstay its welcome like a lot of pop trash on the radio these days. At three minutes into the track we get one of the most profound things Madonna has ever done in music: one second of pure silence. Then her voice emerges from the silence with the line, "If I ran away," after which the music starts up again as if trying to catch her. Her voice drifts upward on that same line, "If I ran away," in a floating freedom that is wonderful to hear. Given the turn to bitmapping, overdubbing, and sampling everything to the point of making a song the equivalent of an oversized Big Mac, there is something in that one second of silence that brings a line like "If I ran away" into such relief that even twenty-five years later I can still feel it.

### The Clash—"London Calling"

Sometimes what it means to love is to become an activist for the sake of those without voice and without power. Too often love is translated as a passivity of comfort, a waiting to embrace those who are hurt and wounded yet without the advocacy to stand up, speak out, and liberate the downtrodden. It is in this way that The Clash made some of pop music's most important modern love songs.

In 1976, when I was eleven years old, my school took a field trip to see a touring exhibition called "The Freedom Train." This was a celebration tour of the United States bicentennial where restored steam locomotives toured the 48 continental states as a rolling museum showcasing American history. Inside the train were a number of American artifacts including Abraham Lincoln's stovepipe hat, George Washington's copy of the Constitution, the original Louisiana Purchase, Judy Garland's dress from *The Wizard of Oz*, Joe Frazier's boxing trunks, and Martin Luther King Jr.'s pulpit and robes. My class waited *hours* in line just to board the train and walk through the various cars for thirty minutes of Americana. I think I had my Steve Martin "I'm a Wild and Crazy Guy" T-shirt on for the occasion. Yet what was occurring *outside* the Freedom Train in the country that gave birth to ours during that fabled summer of '76 remains with me just as much.

During that summer, two centuries after the Declaration of Independence, a new band formed in London that rode the wave of the punk scene and went beyond it, taking punk into the mainstream while being true to its roots. Mick Jones, Paul Simonon, and Keith Levene were looking to do something different, trying to move music forward with the edgy attack of the Sex Pistols. What they found was an aggressive kid named Joe Strum-

mer who was fronting a bar band called the 101ers. They recruited Terry
Chimes for drums and rock history added a new name: The Clash.

I didn't get into The Clash until later; there were too many singer-
songwriters in my diet at the time. It wasn't until I was in seminary and
studying liberation theology that the connection happened. Liberation
theology is a reading of Jesus' mission as described in terms of liberation,
with Jesus as a bringer of justice. This is interpreted as a call to arms—
sometimes literally—in order to carry out Christ's mission of justice. It is
an activist interpretation, one that contrasts with the passivist interpretation of Jesus as Redeemer, which leaves devout Christians as passive
receivers of divine redemption and of the earthly status quo. I remember a
guy in my class saying, "You know, Gustavo Gutierrez could have written
'The Guns of Brixton' on *London Calling*." So I went to Tower Records and
picked up *London Calling* and then saw, that is, *heard*, what can happen
when a band embodying radical passion, idealism, and political social
zeal blends that impulse with punk, reggae, hip-hop, and funk—a smor-
gasbord of sources drawn from the margins of pop radio in the late 1970s,
when the Bee Gees were still selling millions of records.

The title song on *London Calling* announces that "War is declared and
battle come down." It warns against pushing off our responsibility in this
life by just turning into fans and expecting The Clash to take care of things
alone: "Now don't look to us / Phoney Beatlemania has bitten the dust."
The song draws a bleak picture of the times—"The ice age is coming, the
sun's zooming in / Engines stop running, the wheat is growing thin"—but
calls on us as listeners to come out of our drugged-out, overly entertained
stupor and take up the fight for the voiceless, without constantly looking
to big-city power brokers (London) or the rich and famous (The Clash
themselves) for cues. "Forget it, brother, we can go it alone / Quit holding
out and draw another breath / I don't wanna shout / But while we were
talking I saw you nodding out."

If there was ever a time to take seriously the straight edge of punk as
a methodology for what the church and theology are about, it's now. Take
a listen to The Clash again and let's "rock the casbah."

### The Hold Steady—"How a Resurrection Really Feels"

As I was driving to work one morning I heard a snippet of the first
single from The Hold Steady's album *Stay Positive*, called "Sequestered
in Memphis." At first I thought I was listening to KEXP 90.3, an indie

radio station in Seattle that I had heard play earlier Hold Steady songs and is known for playing music outside the mainstream. When I looked at the tuner in my car, I saw, to my horror, that the song was playing on (gulp) NPR's *All Things Considered*! As the song moved from its refrain, *Morning Edition*'s Steve Inskeep continued his interview with lead singer Craig Finn.

Granted, I am happy for Finn and company to get the exposure they rightly deserve as one of the best bands in America at present, and I hope the sales of *Stay Positive* rocket through the roof. But, as with most things we hold dear in life, the more people discover a secret, the less powerful it is. Think of that favorite café you go to when you need some space to think. (I have mine; it's in Seattle's First Hill neighborhood.) Think of that shoebox you kept under the bed as a kid, the one filled with the treasures you never wanted your parents or siblings to find—notes from camp, green army men you melted with a magnifying glass at a friend's house, baseball cards, a crumpled picture of Kristy McNichol from some forgotten ABC afterschool special, and the rest. There are some bands that hold that kind of place. U2 was like that in the early 80s for me. When Christian kids "got serious" about their faith in those days, they abandoned all music except what was sanctioned by the CCM machine (burn The Beatles' albums, buy Amy Grant). But I got more out of U2's *War*—and still do—than I ever did from Petra or White Heart.

I think The Hold Steady will have such a place for another generation. Perhaps they won't move on to fill stadiums and rebrand African poverty like Bono and the boys have done, but Craig Finn's lyrics and the band's bar-busting song craft have certainly added a much-needed element to Christian engagement with the world that is sorely missing from a majority of CCM pabulum in three big ways: honesty, humanity, and a conviction that, for many people, God is more often found in the everyday than in the transcendent.

As Craig Finn states in relation to the band's 2005 album *Separation Sunday*, much of their music is about real people finding real redemption. In his *All Things Considered* interview, Finn called the collection "a prodigal-daughter story." "It is about a girl who grew up in a religious background and goes off to try to find something bigger, better, or something she's missing. And [she] has a lot of experiences and ends up coming back, not only to her family and to her town, but to her church."[11]

11. Inskeep, "The Hold Steady."

This "coming back" story that weaves its way through the album is a gritty account of a girl named Holly ("Her parents named her Hallelujah / The kids all called her Holly") who lives the life of disappointment and heartbreak many people in middle-class America live out every day but rarely admit to—drugs on the side table at bedtime, drinking to get slightly drunk and forget the disappointments of life, relationships that are merely sexual encounters without love. What makes Finn's Holly such an important voice for the church today is that she can actually teach us something if the church will listen. For many CCM artists, redemption results in the ability to conform to our consumer culture rather than to transform it. Being "redeemed" is in the mode of redeeming a coupon clipped from the newspaper, a game of giving up one thing in order to buy another. For Finn, it is not the type of coupon clipping depicted in the connect-the-dots redemption stories so often heard by the third verse of CCM songs. In the closing song of *Separation Sunday*, the aptly titled "How a Resurrection Really Feels," Finn's prodigal daughter stumbles into a church service:

> If she scared you then she's sorry.
> She's been stranded at these parties.
> These parties they start lovely
> But they get druggy and they get ugly
> And they get bloody.
> The priest just kinda laughed. The deacon caught a draft.
> She crashed into the Easter Mass with her hair done up in
>    broken glass.
> She was limping left on broken heels.
> When she said "Father, can I tell your congregation how a
>    Resurrection really feels?"

Where most CCM is only understood and therefore purchased by devoted Christians, Finn's real-life redemption strips away the abstractions and makes redemption something that real people want—something they can experience and still remain real people. On their album *Stay Positive*, the band pens one of the more horrific songs of students away at college I have ever heard, called "One for the Cutters." For a generation that saw the 1979 indie film *Breaking Away*, the image of Indiana University and the town of Bloomington is still alive with a town divided between the "Cutters" (the townies whose families cut the limestone from the surrounding quarries) and the college kids who view them apart from amidst their frat houses and golden futures. Finn reimagines this clash of cultures in Bloomington with a young college student who gets involved with a "Cutter" and with one bad move changes her life forever. The question posed by Finn at the end of this tale will cause cell phones to ring at midnight in dorms across the country:

> Mom, do you know where your girl is?
> Sophomore accomplice in a turtleneck sweater
> Dad, do you know where your kids are?
> Sniffing on crystal in cute little cars
> It's a cute little town, boutiques and cafés
> Her friends all seemed nice, she was getting good grades
> But when she came home for Christmas, she just seemed distant
>     and different.

That "distant and different" is ignored by many in hopes that we can just "move on." Moving on isn't something The Hold Steady offers. As real people, we all live with the scars of our past. Where much of CCM is more concerned with getting past the brokenness and into the light, Finn does the gospel thing instead by shining a light on the brokenness and sitting there for a while with us. It is the unblinking and steady realism that has brought The Hold Steady comparisons to Bruce Springsteen and Bob Dylan—a willingness to say it like it is, not merely how we wish it were. In this way, The Hold Steady live into their name, a band that "holds the gaze," as both Maurice Blanchot and Jacques Lacan describe, and the listener is held to the power and the glory of our real lives that are still in need of real redemption.

All this ruminating on redemption amidst beer parties and murder scenes can lead one to think that the band is destined to be the religious torchbearer of the alt-rock scene. That might come to pass, but I doubt it. This is no Icarus band seeking to take flight and escape the world on waxen wings by soaring into the abstract. When NPR's Steve Inskeep asked him if he thought all his reflection on spiritual matters might result in his becoming like Cat Stevens—moving away from music and into the mystical—Finn said, "I think I'm more religious than spiritual. I don't know if I'm that spiritual a person; I just like going to church. I wonder if I might [be] the opposite of Cat Stevens and then be too normal and end up watching too many baseball games and eating too many hot wings."[12]

12. Ibid.

If Finn's lyrics are anything like his conversations, I would join him for a bucket of hot wings at the ballgame after church anytime.

### Cat Stevens—"How Can I Tell You?"

The end of my school's academic quarter breeds a high level of malaise, that feeling of wandering in a cloud and being damp with sadness. Is this merely due to reading too much Sartre, Camus, and Heidegger? *Aucun je ne pense pas ainsi*—that is, no, I don't think so.

That said, the ending of the term, the drama of grades, and the fear of seniors not knowing what comes next certainly adds to this anxiety. I was listening to Cat Stevens's album *Teaser and the Firecat* one afternoon and was thinking about this simple ode to love in relation to the momentary anxiety we find ourselves in. Long before bands like Mumford and Sons, Fleet Foxes, The Shins, and Kings of Convenience there was Cat Stevens, *née* Yusaf Islam. "How Can I Tell You?" is a love song so filled with longing and loss that it pours out of your speakers. In some ways the song is so intimate that it can't be listened to with earbuds—too closed and intimate, and like a good wine it has to breathe a bit. The song begins in silence and you sit for four painful seconds waiting for something, anything, to fill it. Then enters the first strum of the guitar and the fingerpicking that is seeking for the form of the narrative. Stevens's voice only stumbles into the song after twenty-one seconds, which, in a song three minutes and eighteen seconds long, can feel like an eternity. He hums and tries to awaken his language around his longing and then begins with his question: "How can I tell you that I love you?" From there the song falls in and out of metaphors—seeing the face of his beloved in every face he tries to love, the phasing in and out of the sea on the shoreline—each metaphor trying to give some grounding to this longing that is slowly drawing him into the distance. After three minutes a quiet wailing fills the background of the song and his voice falls off into silence once again. It is jarring to listen to the song all the way into the next track, "Tuesday's Dead," which, while a great track, is abruptly upbeat in tone. I wonder why the many greatest hits collections never include "How Can I Tell You?" ("Tuesday's Dead" makes it on the A&M collection) but perhaps the reason is obvious: How can this level of raw transparency be something that folks want to return to? One of the gifts of being a pastor that I still am confounded by is the gift of those moments when someone is in my office seeking at first some answer to a question, a concern, or a disturbance in their logic, and inevitably the questions that seemed so pressing fade to the background as tears begin to flow, their shoulders begin to shake, and we are back to the most basic of concerns: Am I loved? Time and time again it comes down to this question for people—in the careers they choose, in the friends they seek out, in the romances they long for, in the God that they find so elusive. The struggle against loneliness, the desire to laugh freely with someone who they trust with the fragility of joy, the passions to be embraced and dreams to be shared. Over and over the question of how we can tell someone else that we desire to love them and have a deep desire to be loved haunts the back corners of everyone's soul, even the successful CEO, the Hollywood celebrity, the beautiful model, and the strong athlete. It is a constant that in many ways has fueled the drug trade, the Freudian revolution, the consumer drive of capitalism, the blockbuster film industry, and the pocketbooks of self-help gurus, and is the sustaining chord that rings down the canyons of time. With this being such a vital question, perhaps it is time that the church took love seriously once again.

## Grateful Dead—"Friend of the Devil"

Listening to music is akin to the various forms that water takes as it moves from steam to liquid to ice. We encounter music in one context, yet when the song is moved into a different context it can seem that we have heard that song before, but we do not recognize it. Something new arises that allows the same chords, singers, and time signature to seem completely new. Listening to a Grateful Dead recording and then moving that song into the world that is a Dead show is a grand example. After I became a Christian in high school, bands like the Grateful Dead represented the sort of pot-hazed indifference to all-that-is-holy that I had been saved from. What I was called to was a life in the church with and for other people where we sought to care for one another, love our neighbors as themselves, and seek after something more than merely living and dying. Where church was held up as the place to find this community, things like rock 'n' roll shows were places of idolatry, hedonism, and self-indulgence, and found their pinnacle in the touring circus of what are known as Deadheads.

Yet in 1993, at the bequest of a good friend who thought I needed to have my eyes and ears opened, I drove my 1970 Orange VW Squareback to the first of two Grateful Dead shows at Autzen Stadium on the campus of the University of Oregon. Having listened to a few Grateful Dead songs in college, I will admit to having been pretty underwhelmed at first listen. Sure, the Haight-Ashbury scene of 1960s San Francisco, with bands like the Mamas and the Papas, Jefferson Airplane, and Janis Joplin, which rolled into pop culture on the back of the Beat poets of the late 50s, was a seismic cultural event and set the stage for much of what is called the singer-songwriter movement. From coffeehouses to flower power and reaching an apex with the "summer of love" in 1967 after the Monterey Pop Festival, I certainly thought the whole vibe was great and all, but having hardened to the idealism of "flower power" with the reality of needing to get my student loans paid, I accepted the fact that sometimes you just need to get a job and go to work, and sitting around in coffee shops wasn't going to pay the rent. And so in my late 20s I entered the world of the Deadheads and found out how wrong I was. Sure, the Grateful Dead is essentially a B-league Country Western band at best, with only a couple of hit singles after decades of making music, but the experience of going to a Dead show is something that everyone hopes church will be like and rarely is.

The first thing you notice are the people holding cardboard signs on the street outside the show venue with the phrase "One miracle" scrawled on it—a reference to their song "I Need a Miracle," which has the refrain "I need a miracle everyday"—in hopes of scoring a ticket to the show. What is amazing is that, as opposed to people scalping tickets right and left, people will just give their ticket to someone holding a sign. Also, people sitting in the parking lot at the show formed the equivalent of a tailgate party thrown by organic farmers—rows of blankets set out with apples, oranges, and free poetry for the taking. One person was making toasted cheese sandwiches on his engine block, which, once you get past the oil and dirt, isn't half bad. Once inside the venue the show is truly a three-ring interactive circus—people milling around throughout the songs, people offering you bottled water and dried fruit, asking where you came from and if you need a ride after the show.

In front of the stage you would see hundreds of poles with microphones taped to them to record the show. The Grateful Dead were truly one of the first "open source" bands, letting people record their shows and share them as they wished. Where bootlegged music was always an illegal affair, picking up copies of Dead shows on cassette tape was a regular and open occasion at every show and a way that fans "passed the peace" with one another—handing off copies of shows that people missed as a way to keep friends in the loop and updating what was on the set list the past tour season. All throughout the shows you would see a group of people in front of the stage called "spinners" who would give themselves over to the music and, well, spin to their hearts' delight akin to the Sufi whirling dervishes. Given the fact that many Dead shows lasted four to six hours, this was a physical feat to behold. Where many church worship services try to focus your attention at all times and leave little to no room for reflection and contemplation, every Dead show included a prolonged drum solo by drummer Mickey Hart and Bill Kreutzmann called "space," which would go on for almost a half an hour, where people would mingle, talk, dance their hearts out, be silent amidst the rhythm, and wonder what was yet to come.

Blair Jackson, in his biography of lead singer Jerry Garcia, pointed out that Dead shows were not just rock shows coupled with drugs, but were something that thousands of people found community and acceptance in. Jackson went so far as to state that the "shows were the sacrament . . . rich and full of blissful, transcendent musical moments that moved the body and enriched the soul."[13] The religious nature of Dead shows was not lost on the band members. Citing Mickey Hart, Jackson notes that the gatherings in concerts were literally creating a space where people could be moved into another way of living, stating that "the Grateful Dead weren't in the music business, they were in the *transportation* business. For many Deadheads, the band was a medium that facilitated experiencing other planes of consciousness and tapping into deep, spiritual wells that were usually the province of organized religion."[14]

Suffice it to say, I am not saying that a Dead show was heaven on earth. Yes, there was a lot of pot smoke floating around and regular hygiene practices were something of a novelty for many Deadheads. But the generosity of spirit in a crowd of 30,000 was truly a wonder to behold. As a statement of what love is all about, this movement of boundless hospitality, embrace of anyone, and friendship for the journey was something I will never forget and wish I saw more examples of inside of churches these days. Many big-box churches have massive parking lots so that people can come and go in the privacy of their own cars. As opposed to people standing around expecting a "miracle," few of the people I sit next to in churches today would know a miracle if it came up and shook their hand, and I put myself in that category as well. Making a community through what we

13. Jackson, *Garcia*, 219.
14. Ibid., 319.

can give away—our food, our art, a place in our car, or the water from my water bottle—as opposed to what we get out of it is something that many churches could do well to try out as a missions model.

One of the songs the Grateful Dead are best known for is "Friend of the Devil," which was the second track off one of their 1970s albums entitled *American Beauty*. The protagonist in the song is an outlaw who is running from both the law and the devil. The outlaw continues to run throughout the song and you are never sure if it is Satan or the law who is the bigger problem. He laments his loss of family and just wants to get home before daylight. One thing that the outlaw learns is that the journey to daylight is best run with others, as the chorus states, "I set out running but I'm taking my time/ A friend of the devil is a friend of mine." I used to take that to mean that the song celebrated Satanists or some other occult darkness, but after going to a Dead show I see it from a very different angle. The protagonist in the song is running and those who are chasing him—be it the devil or the law—have already summed up both his fate and his motivations and therefore damned him from the start. To those singing along with lead singer Jerry Garcia, anyone who has been pushed to the margins and judged as being damned even before asking what constitutes salvation are those that some segments of the Christian subculture have deemed "friends of the devil." Interestingly, the term "heathen" is one that arises from a view that people who lived outside of the cities—the centers of power and knowledge—and took up residence on the *heath* were obviously lost from God and were therefore designated "heathens." And yet so many of these "heathens" are finding communities of meaning, seeking after the welfare of the lost and lonely, and giving what they have to support others. If those who are outcasts only find friendship with the devil because the churches around them have closed their doors and silenced their music, what are we do? Perhaps we are to hitch a ride, accept the miracle offered to us, see where the next show is, break bread with our neighbor with a slice of dried fruit and cup of water, and dance till we drop. Maybe we will see that perhaps the devil doesn't have all the good music after all, and those we had thought to be friends of the enemy were our neighbors all along—those we are called to love as ourselves, and share music with.

# 5

# Bonus Track

### From Hearing to Seeing to Singing

A S YOU HAVE JOURNEYED through these various pop songs and the
artists who created them, I hope that you have arrived at a new place
in relation to what is happening in the world of pop music and a renewed
humility as to the ways that matters of the heart, mind, and soul get si-
multaneously formed and ignited even in the simplest pop song. Many
people begin the journey of seeking after what is meaningful and deep in
this life with what others would consider as the most mundane or even
vile and repulsive.

Going back to the question of what it means to have faith, we are to
remember that to have faith in something is to essentially stand upon it,
to trust it with your heart, mind, and soul. The word translated as "faith"
in the Greek New Testament is *pistis*, which is the root word from which
we derive "epistemology," which in philosophy is the study of what we believe to be so true that everything else depends on it. In science we begin
with a premise, theory, or idea that we test and retest through controlled
experiments and the result is often a "proof," some statement that (bar-
ring any countervailing evidence that may arise) stands now as proven.
Such proof statements in the past have included the following:

The world is flat.

The sun rotates around the earth given that the earth is the center of
the universe.

(and one of my favorites . . .)

Pluto is a planet.[1]

Now, I don't want to spoil this for you, but most people in the scientific community have "proven" that these proof statements listed above are no longer valid and to "have faith" in these statements is problematic. Whether these proof statements are true or false really doesn't have a lot of impact on my day-to-day life. True, I might think twice about boarding a ship sailing westward if I thought it would sail off the end of the world, but it doesn't actually cost me much if these are true or false. Which is why I don't have faith in them one way or another. Because, ultimately, faith is that which everything depends on. It is a life-and-death issue, not merely a question of whether that large rock rotating on the outer part of our solar system is a "planet," "dwarf planet," or "plutinoid" as some have called it.

Throughout the Gospel of John to have faith is the direct response to the self-disclosure of the singular and unique representative of God, who alone illuminates and bears life, and life abundantly. This illumination for faith is seen by people (1) making the right sounds that will cause us to see the world differently and move us from darkness into light, (2) honestly testifying (bearing witness) to what they see because of the light, and (3) choosing to not merely see, but live according to this witness in every aspect of their lives by now singing a new song into the culture in which they find themselves.

## THE FIRST MOVEMENT OF FAITH:
## HEARING THE SOUND THAT CAUSES US TO SEE
## AND MOVE FROM DARKNESS INTO LIGHT

"Light" is one of the most widely used images in religions around the world and throughout history, and it affirms the human appeal for God. The use of φως (*phos*, "light") is significant in John's Gospel—twenty-three occurrences in the Gospel of John and six in 1 John among the seventy-three total New Testament occurrences. Light is characteristic of epiphany narratives (theophanies and angelophanies: Matt 17:2; Acts 9: 3; 22:6, 9, 11; 26:13). Light is also represented in the divine power of God's

1. For those who are interested in the fate of poor Pluto, on August 24, 2006, the International Astronomical Union (IAU) defined the term "planet" for the first time. This definition excluded Pluto as a planet due to the fact that larger bodies were found. RIP Pluto.

liberation of captives (Acts 12: 7; 16:29). 1 Timothy 6:16 employs the image of light as one of Judaism's traditional attributes of God, portraying him as one "who dwells in unapproachable light" and thus cannot be seen directly by human beings. The categories of light and darkness belong to a ubiquitous language of world religions. For example, Gnosticism, which developed in the dualistic systems of Manichaeism and Mandaism, was in effect a "religion of light" where light and darkness were seen as independent opposing powers. The use of the images of light and darkness is seen as appealing to the author's formerly pagan readers with the image of light prominent in Greek thinking. Yet, the image of light in the Old Testament is used in an intellectual sense to show truth, and darkness to show error and evil, and therefore would have spoken to a Jewish audience as well as a Hellenistic one.

Jesus states in John 9:5 as he approaches a man born blind, "While I am in the world, I am the light of the world" (NIV). John's Gospel is filled with instances of Jesus identifying himself as the "I AM" (*ego eimi* in the Greek), which is the self-identification YHWH gives to Moses in Exodus 3:14 as he stands before the light of the ever-burning bush: "I AM WHO I AM. This is what you are to say to the Israelites: 'I AM has sent me to you.'" Here in John 9, the "I AM" is the *phos* of everything (ὅταν ἐν τῷ κόσμῳ ὦ, φῶς εἰμι τοῦ κόσμου)—not merely of the world, but the whole *cosmos* . . . even poor Pluto! This grand light of faith—that which makes the cosmos makes sense—encounters this man who has never seen with his own eyes and now can see.

For students immersed in Koine Greek in our seminary program, when you take New Testament Greek one of the first words you learn is the word for "to see" or "sight"—*blepō*. In part this is because "to see" is so prevalent throughout the New Testament that you feel like you are getting somewhere to learn it (and in part because it just sounds hysterical to say *blepō* all the time).

### THIS BRINGS US TO THE SECOND MOVE OF FAITH: HONESTLY TESTIFYING (BEARING WITNESS) TO WHAT YOU SEE BECAUSE OF THE LIGHT

So Jesus "*blepos*" this man and he now sees. But he not only sees, he also testifies to the fact. He is now the placeholder for Jesus in front of other people. In 9:9, when people see him he is no longer begging and they wonder whether it is the one they knew as "the blind man." The man states rather resolutely that not only *was* he the one born blind, he is now "I AM" in a representative way. The Greek in the verse is translated in the NIV as "he himself insisted 'I am the man.'" In actuality, as Greek grammar geeks will point out, there is no predicate for the subject of the sentence, which is one way of saying that he isn't defined by anything anymore. He is not "the man," "the formerly blind guy," or even "the healed guy." No, he is ἐγὼ εἰμι—or "I AM" in their presence. No more labels, no more using the compass points of culture to make sense of what is valued and what isn't. No, this encounter so radically shifted the man that he simply is who he is and was always meant to be—himself. "I am that I am."

When I think about this amazing shift in John 9—one who was blind but now has been given sight in such a dramatic way—I am reminded of the poem by the Nobel laureate Pablo Neruda that describes what it was like for him to write creatively for the first time in the last lines of his poem "Poetry":

> And I, infinitesimal being, drunk with the great starry void, like-
> ness, image of mystery, felt myself a pure part of the abyss,
>
> > I wheeled with the stars
>
> > and my heart broke free on the open sky.[2]

Have you ever been around people who have this type of experience? Wheeling in the stars and their heart broken free on the open sky? As I reflected upon in regard to watching the spinners at a Grateful Dead show, it is spellbinding to say the least.

This was certainly the case for those who interrogated the man in the rest of John 9, pushing him to frame his experience in ways that made sense to them—the models of belief that they were comfortable with, using the stories that they grew up with and not some seemingly new story of faith, saying the right thing for his family so that the family would not have to change, so that things would stay just like they always have been.

### Pleasantville—Separating Out That Which Is Pleasant from That Which Is Unpleasant

There is something in this exchange with the man born blind that is similar to a scene in the 1998 film *Pleasantville*. In the movie Tobey

---

2. Neruda, "Poetry," in *Essential Neruda*, 169.

Maguire plays a teenager named David obsessed with a 1950s TV show called *Pleasantville*. His life is a mess—his parents' marriage is dissolving around him, he doesn't fit into his school—and he pines for a basic world of black and white (both figuratively and literally) to escape into. He is thrown into this black-and-white TV world and at first loves how certain everything is—no shades of grey, just black and white. But slowly he begins to ask questions, to seek to know more in a world where people don't want things to change. People start to have color where things were black and white, and this idealized, safe TV world must decide whether it will change or cast out color in favor of black-and-white certainty. One of the town leaders, wonderfully named "Big Bob," holds a meeting in the town bowling alley (because, as he says, "Nothing will hurt us here because nothing ever changes in a bowling alley") and states:

> Up until now everything around here has been, well, pleasant. Recently certain things have become unpleasant. Now, it seems to me that the first thing we have to do is to separate out the things that are pleasant from the things that are unpleasant.

This is essentially what is happening in John with the interrogation of the man born blind—stating that things that are unpleasant have no place in true religion, so we should separate out that which is pleasant from that which is unpleasant.

## THIS BRINGS US TO THE THIRD MOVEMENT OF FAITH: CHOOSING TO NOT MERELY SEE, BUT TO LIVE ACCORDING TO THIS WITNESS IN EVERY ASPECT OF LIFE

In Habakkuk 2:4 the prophet reminds us of this important point: the righteous will live by faith. Probably one of the most important adages in all of Christian theology, this commission is used in Romans 1:17, Galatians 3:11, and Hebrews 10:38 as the starting point of the concept of faith. It is this verse reframed in Romans 1:17 that stopped the German Augustinian monk Martin Luther in his tracks and forged a direction that would result in the challenging of one established form of faith and help usher in a new day. It was this same verse amidst the growing madness of early-twentieth-century Europe as it lived in fear after World War I and saw the rise of National Socialism and the Nazi party, that brought a young Swiss church preacher named Karl Barth to write *Der Römerbrief*

("Commentary on the Epistle to the Romans") in 1922 to question whether people were taking seriously the role that sin plays in our lives and that the cross of Christ is the only hope for a world trusting in the certainty of regimes and propaganda machines; this work has changed the way Protestant churches read the Scriptures some ninety years later. These two of the most significant shifts (not only for the church but the world at large) were forged into being because someone took seriously the notion that faith is not only seeing what is real, but testifying to others about that reality and living it out fully with one's whole life. In the end, the man born blind cannot say what or how or why his miracle occurred. All he can offer, as we hear in verse 9:25, is that "I was blind but now I see!"

As this section of Scripture closes, the man is thrown out into the street and Jesus—now thirty verses after giving the man sight and the longest passage in the Gospels where Jesus is completely absent—shows up and asks if he has faith. In verse 9:35 Jesus asks the man, "Do you believe [*pistis* = faith] in the Son of Man?" The man replies in the next verse that he wants to have faith . . . but he doesn't know where to put it yet—"Who is he [the Son of Man], sir?" the man asked. "Tell me so that I may believe [*pistis* = faith] in him." Jesus then lays the cards on the table: "You have now seen [*blepo*] him, in fact, he is the one speaking to you" (v. 37). "Then the man said, 'Lord, I believe [*pistis* = faith]," and he worshipped him" (v. 38).

What is missing from this powerful exchange is a clear, concise articulation of what faith actually means in the form that is often spoken of in many churches—no adherence to a particular doctrine, no perfunctory liturgical strategy, no catechism nor membership class to seal the deal. Something happened. The man had faith in it. He knew one basic thing: that his life would never be the same. Jesus showed up and was worshipped. And the canon of Scripture holds this to be a sacred moment. How is this different from the types of encounters with some pop songs that we have discussed throughout this book thus far? Sure, regaining physical eyesight trumps going to a really rocking concert, but for some people it will be pretty close. That one song that pushes us through the mundane to the transcendent can be akin to having our eyes opened to faith, hope, and love for the very first time. Like Neruda's encounter with poetry, we may not have words at first and will play that silly song over and over again in a futile attempt to capture lightening in a bottle and hold fast to this luminous moment. Faith is like that for many people, and we may interrogate them to get specifics, cast them out as "people of the heath" and label them as "friends of the devil" when we don't hear what we want to hear. But we also need to be ready to find that Jesus is waiting out there for them while we argue inside. If we would have faith to follow our neighbors out into the highways and byways, perhaps we too would be surprised by who we find waiting and what songs they would have us sing.

## VEDRAN SMAILOVIĆ—FAITH AS PLAYING ONE NOTE AT A TIME

In 1992 at the height of the Bosnian conflict, Vedran Smailović, a member of the Sarajevo Opera Orchestra, while waiting in a breadline at a bakery, lost twenty-two friends to mortar fire that destroyed the bakery as well as continued shelling that destroyed the opera house. For twenty-two days this lone cellist dressed in full evening tails, sat in a burned chair found in rubble, and continued to play his cello on the streets of Sarajevo in the shadow of violence. When asked by a CNN reporter if he was not crazy for playing his cello while Sarajevo was being shelled, Smailović replied, "You ask me if am I crazy for playing the cello, why do you not ask if they are crazy for shelling Sarajevo?"[3]

As a member of the Sarajevo Opera Orchestra, there is little he could do about hate and war since it had been going on in Sarajevo for centuries. Even so, every day for twenty-two days he sat there doing what he knew—bringing beauty into the world in the face of sniper and artillery fire. His chosen piece? Albinoni's profoundly moving *Adagio in G Minor*, which itself is a survivor of war—Albinoni constructed the piece from a manuscript fragment found in the ruins of Dresden after the Second World War. Here is music that survived the firebombing and found yet another life in the hands of Vedran Smailović in the scarred streets of Sarajevo, where people died waiting in line for bread. Is this man crazy? Maybe. Is his gesture futile? Yes, in a conventional sense, of course. But sometimes we are only left with music, and perhaps that is what we are left with now as we end this meditation on pop music. One note at a time can change the world around us. Yes, there is madness in the world, but there is also faith and hope and love. Maybe it is insane and frivolous to sit and play a song when people are in poverty and struggling to survive.

3. Green, *Mastery of Music*, 119.

But perhaps it is insane to keep silent and forget that even the simplest song that lifts the burden of darkness for a spell can let enough light in to illuminate not only the eyes of one formerly blind man, but restore vision and hope to a generation.

What will your song be? What song offers a reason to sing in the streets, to dance in the midst of despair, and to share with others because a slice of your life resides there? Turn up the volume a little bit and let people into your playlist. You might be surprised what your neighbour will say and what you have in common after all.

# Bibliography

Abernathy, Luke. "Thoughts On: Fleet Foxes—Fleet Foxes/Sun Giant EP." *The Other Journal*, June 3, 2008. Online: http://www.theotherjournal.com/article.php?id=372.

Abramovich, Alex. "New York in Reverse." *Slate*, October 22, 2003. Online: http://www.slate.com/id/2090203/.

Aichele, George, editor. *Culture, Entertainment and the Bible*. Journal for the Study of the Old Testament, Supplement Series 309. Sheffield: Sheffield Academic, 2000.

Albanese, Catherine L. "Religion and Popular American Culture: An Introductory Essay." *Journal of the American Academy of Religion* 64.4 (1996) 733–42.

Anderson, Walt. *Reality Isn't What It Used to Be: Theatrical Politics, Ready-to-Wear Religion, Global Myths, Primitive Chic and Other Wonders of the Postmodern World*. San Francisco: Harper San Francisco, 1990.

Arthur, Chris, editor. *Religion and the Media: An Introductory Reader*. Cardiff: University of Wales Press, 1993.

Beeaff, Dianne Ebertt. *A Grand Madness: Ten Years on the Road with U2*. Tucson, AZ: Hawkmoon, 2000.

BeingCharlieKaufman.com. "Biography." Online: http://www.beingcharliekaufman.com/index.php?option=com_content&view=article&id=31&Itemid=34.

Blythe, Teresa, and Daniel Wolpert. *Meeting God in Virtual Reality: Using Spiritual Practices with Media*. Nashville: Abingdon, 2004.

Boer, Roland. *Knockin' on Heaven's Door: The Bible and Popular Culture*. Biblical Limits. New York: Routledge, 1999.

Bono. "Bono on Bruce Springsteen." Rock and Roll Hall of Fame. Online: http://rockhall.com/inductees/bruce-springsteen/transcript/bono-on-bruce-springsteen/.

Bordowitz, Hank. *The U2 Reader: A Quarter Century of Commentary, Criticism, and Reviews*. Milwaukee: Hal Leonard, 2003.

Carroll, Cath. *Never Break the Chain: Fleetwood Mac and the Making of Rumours*. London: Unanimous, 2004.

Chidester, David. "The Church of Baseball, the Fetish of Coca-Cola, and the Potlatch of Rock 'N' Roll: Theoretical Models for the Study of Religion in American Popular Culture." *Journal of the American Academy of Religion* 64.4 (1996) 743–65.

Clark, Lynn Schofield. *From Angels to Aliens: Teenagers, the Media, and the Supernatural*. New York: Oxford University Press, 2003.

Cleave, Maureen, "How Does a Beatle Live? John Lennon Lives Like This." *London Evening Standard*, March 4, 1966.

Cochrane, Arthur C. *The Church's Confession under Hitler.* Philadelphia: Westminster, 1962.

Cocks, Jay. "Down to Old Dixie and Back." *Time,* January 12, 1970. Online: http://www .time.com/time/magazine/article/0,9171,942169,00.html.

Coleman, John A., and Miklós Tomka, editors. *Mass Media.* Concilium. Maryknoll, NY: Orbis, 1993.

Cone, James H. *The Spirituals and the Blues: An Interpretation.* New York: Seabury, 1972.

Cross, Charles R. *Heavier than Heaven: A Biography of Kurt Cobain.* New York: Hyperion, 2002.

Crowe, Cameron, writer and director. *Say Anything.* Beverly Hills, CA: Twentieth Century Fox, 1989.

Daddino, Michael. "That Great State: For Singer/Songwriter Sufjan Stevens, God Is in the Details." *Seattle Weekly,* July 20, 2005. Online: http://www.seattleweekly.com/2005-07-20/music/the-great-state.

Detweiler, Craig, and Barry Taylor. *A Matrix of Meanings: Finding God in Pop Culture.* Engaging Culture. Grand Rapids: Baker Academic, 2003.

Detweiler, Linford. "Drunkard's Prayer: Notes." Online: http://www.overtherhine.com/ music/recordings/cd13/cd13c.html

Dodaro, Robert, and John Paul Szura. *Theology and Mass Communication.* Oxford: Blackwell, 1997.

Doe, John. "Biography." 2007. Online: http://www.theejohndoe.com/bio.html.

Doss, Erika Lee. "Saint Elvis." In *Elvis Culture: Fans, Faith, & Image,* 69–113. Lawrence, KS: University Press of Kansas, 1999.

Ewen, Stuart. *All Consuming Images: The Politics of Style in Contemporary Culture.* New York: Basic Books, 1988.

Fagerberg, David W. *Theologia Prima: What Is Liturgical Theology?* Chicago: Hillenbrand, 2004.

Forbes, Bruce David, and Jeffrey H. Mahan, editors. *Religion and Popular Culture in America.* Berkeley: University of California Press, 2000.

Freccero, Carla. *Popular Culture: An Introduction.* New York: New York University Press, 1999.

General Entertainment. "Lee Greenwood." Online: http://www.generalentertainment .com/artists/LeeGreenwood.htm

Gluck, Jeremy S. "Love Untold: St. Paul's Letters to the Philistines." *Bucketfull of Brains,* May 1996.

Gottdiener, Mark. "Dead Elvis as Other Jesus." In *In Search of Elvis: Music, Race, Art, Religion,* edited by Vernon Chadwick, xxvi, 294. Boulder, CO: Westview, 1997.

Gould, Jonathan. *Can't Buy Me Love: The Beatles, Britain, and America.* New York: Harmony, 2007.

Graham, John. "Elliott Smith (1969–2003)." *Willamette Weekly,* October 29th, 2003. Online: http://www.wweek.com/portland/print-article-2607-print.html.

Greeley, Andrew M. *God in Popular Culture.* Chicago: Thomas More, 1988.

Green, Barry. *The Mastery of Music: Ten Pathways to True Artistry.* New York: Broadway, 2003.

Greenwood, Lee. "Bio." Online: http://www.leegreenwood.com/index.php?p=360.

Grimes, William. "The Man Who Rendered Jesus for the Age of Duplication." *New York Times,* October 12, 1994. Online: http://query.nytimes.com/gst/fullpage.html?res=9 D07EEDE163CF931A25753C1A962958260&sec=&spon=&pagewanted=1.

Grossberg, Lawrence. *Dancing in Spite of Myself: Essays on Popular Culture*. Durham, NC: Duke University Press, 1997.

Guder, Darrell L., and Lois Barrett et al, editors. *Missional Church: A Vision for the Sending of the Church in North America*. The Gospel and Our Culture Series. Grand Rapids: Eerdmans, 1998.

Hess, J. Daniel. "Toward a Hermeneutics of Popular Culture." *Conrad Grebel Review* 11.2 (1993) 123–25.

Hibbs, Thomas S. *Shows about Nothing: Nihilism in Popular Culture from The Exorcist to Seinfeld*. Dallas: Spence, 1999.

Hoover, Stewart M., and Knut Lundby, editors. *Rethinking Media, Religion, and Culture*. Thousand Oaks, CA: Sage, 1997.

Hsu, Hua. "Melancholy Arena Rock: Why Is Coldplay Still Depressed?" *Slate*, June 14, 2005. Online: http://www.slate.com/id/2120786/.

Inglis, Fred. *Media Theory: An Introduction*. Cambridge, MA: Blackwell, 1990.

Inskeep, Steve. "The Hold Steady: Rewards and Redemption." *Morning Edition*, July 24, 2008. National Public Radio. Online: http://www.npr.org/templates/story/story.php?storyId=92836913.

Jackson, Blair. *Garcia: An American Life*. New York: Penguin, 1999.

Keys, Alicia. "Marvin Gaye." "100 Greatest Singers of All Time." *Rolling Stone*. Online: http://www.rollingstone.com/music/lists/100-greatest-singers-of-all-time-19691231/marvin-gaye-19691231.

Kitwana, Bakari. *Why White Kids Love Hip-Hop: Wankstas, Wiggers, Wannabes, and the New Reality of Race in America*. New York: Basic Civitas, 2005.

Klotman, Phyllis Rauch. *In Touch with the Spirit: Black Religious and Musical Expression in American Cinema*. Bloomington: Indiana University, 1994.

Lamott, Anne. *Traveling Mercies: Some Thoughts on Faith*. New York: Pantheon, 1999.

Lasch, Christopher. *The Culture of Narcissism: American Life in an Age of Diminishing Expectations*. New York: Norton, 1978.

Loder, James E. *The Transforming Moment: Understanding Convictional Experiences*. New York: Harper & Row, 1981.

Marsh, Dave. *Bruce Springsteen: Two Hearts: The Definitive Biography, 1972–2003*. New York: Routledge, 2004.

Marshall, Scott. *Restless Pilgrim: The Spiritual Journey of Bob Dylan*. Lake Mary, FL: Relevant, 2002.

Masur, Louis P. *Runaway Dream: Born to Run and Bruce Springsteen's American Vision*. New York: Bloomsbury, 2009.

Maynard, Beth. "U2 Live: Where Leitourgia Has No Name." Presented at the "U2: The Hype and the Feedback" conference, North Carolina State University, October 4, 2009.

Mazur, Eric Michael, and Kate McCarthy, editors. *God in the Details: American Religion in Popular Culture*. New York: Routledge, 2001.

McDannell, Colleen. *Material Christianity: Religion and Popular Culture in America*. New Haven, CT: Yale University Press, 1995.

McLuhan, Marshall. *Understanding Media: The Extensions of Man*. New York: McGraw-Hill, 1964.

Miller, Vincent Jude. *Consuming Religion: Christian Faith and Practice in a Consumer Culture*. New York: Continuum, 2004.

Mitchell, Jolyon P., and Sophia Marriage. *Mediating Religion: Conversations in Media, Religion and Culture*. New York: T. & T. Clark, 2003.

Moltmann, Jürgen. *Theology of Hope: On the Ground and the Implications of a Christian Eschatology*. Translated by James W. Leitch. Minneapolis: Fortress, 1993.

Monk, Paul. "Under the Spell of Stranger Music: Leonard Cohen's Lyrical Judaism." *Australian Financial Review*, June 8, 2001. Online: http://www.leonardcohenfiles .com/paulmonk.html.

Morgan, David. *Visual Piety: A History and Theory of Popular Religious Images*. Berkeley: University of California Press, 1998.

Myers, Kenneth A. *All God's Children and Blue Suede Shoes: Christians & Popular Culture*. Turning Point Christian Worldview Series. Westchester, IL: Crossway, 1989.

Neruda, Pablo. *The Essential Neruda: Selected Poems*. Edited by Mark Eisner, translated by Mark Eisner et al. San Francisco: City Lights, 2004.

Nietzsche, Frederick. *Thus Spoke Zarathustra*. In *The Portable Nietzsche*, translated by Walter Kaufmann. New York: Viking, 1954. Reprint, New York: Penguin, 1982.

Petridis, Alexis. "The Mysterious Death of Mr. Misery." *The Guardian*, March 19, 2004. Online: http://www.guardian.co.uk/music/2004/mar/19/popandrock.elliottsmith.

Postman, Neil. *Amusing Ourselves to Death: Public Discourse in the Age of Show Business*. New York: Viking, 1985.

Reed, Teresa L. *The Holy Profane: Religion in Black Popular Music*. Lexington: University of Kentucky Press, 2003.

Romanowski, William D. "'You Talkin' to Me?' The Christian Liberal Arts Tradition and the Challenge of Popular Culture." In *Keeping the Faith: Embracing the Tensions in Christian Higher Education*, edited by Ronald A. Wells, 106–32. Grand Rapids: Eerdmans, 1996.

———. *Eyes Wide Open: Looking for God in Popular Culture*. Grand Rapids: Brazos, 2001.

Rossi, Philip J., and Paul A. Soukup, editors. *Mass Media and the Moral Imagination*. Communication, Culture & Theology. Kansas City: Sheed & Ward, 1994.

Sample, Tex. *White Soul: Country Music, the Church, and Working Americans*. Nashville: Abingdon, 1996.

Schmemann, Alexander. *For the Life of the World*. Crestwood NY: St. Vladimir's Seminary Press, 1973.

Schultze, Quentin J. *Dancing in the Dark: Youth, Popular Culture, and the Electronic Media*. Grand Rapids: Eerdmans, 1991.

Seling, Megan. "Fleet Foxes Are Not Hippies." *The Stranger*, January 30, 2008. Online: http://www.thestranger.com/seattle/Content?oid=496329.

Shelton, Robert. *No Direction Home: The Life and Music of Bob Dylan*. Cambridge, MA: Da Capo, 1997.

Springsteen, Bruce, and Dave Diomedi, director. *VH1 Storytellers: Bruce Springsteen*. DVD. Sony BMG, 2005.

Sragow, Michael. "Being Charlie Kaufman." *Salon*, November 11, 1999. Online: http:// www.salon.com/entertainment/col/srag/1999/11/11/kaufman/index.html.

Stout, Daniel A., and Judith Mitchell Buddenbaum, editors. *Religion and Mass Media: Audiences and Adaptations*. Thousand Oaks, CA: Sage, 1996.

Turner, Steve. *Hungry for Heaven: Rock 'n' Roll and the Search for Redemption*. Downers Grove, IL: InterVarsity, 1996.

Viladesau, Richard. *Theology and the Arts: Encountering God through Music, Art, and Rhetoric*. New York: Paulist, 2000.

Wald, Elijah. *How the Beatles Destroyed Rock 'n' Roll: An Alternative History of American Popular Music.* New York: Oxford University Press, 2009.

Warren, Michael. *Seeing through the Media: A Religious View of Communication and Cultural Analysis.* Harrisburg, PA: Trinity, 1997.

Whiteley, Raewynne J., and Beth Maynard. *Get Up off Your Knees: Preaching the U2 Catalog.* Cambridge, MA: Cowley, 2003.

Whittle, Donald Carey Grenfell. *Christianity and the Arts.* London: Mowbray, 1966.

Zimmerman, Kevin. "Snow Patrol." *MusicWorld*, March 9, 2005. BMI. Online: http://www.bmi.com/news/entry/234372.

# Discography

## FAITH

Mitchell, Joni. "God Must Be a Boogie Man." *Mingus*. Ⓟ 1979 Elektra/Asylum Records, B00002GWV.

Blue Scholars. "Burnt Offering." *Blue Scholars*. Ⓟ 2004 MASSLine Records, B000E6UKK0.

Metallica. "Nothing Else Matters." *Metallica*. Ⓟ 1991 Elektra Records, B00003XAVX.

Vigilantes of Love. "Double Cure." *V.O.L.* Ⓟ 1996 Warner Bros., B000002N9F.

Nirvana. "Smells Like Teen Spirit." *Nevermind*. Ⓟ 1991 Geffen Records, B000003TA4.

Cash, Johnny. *My Mother's Hymnbook*. Ⓟ 2004 American Recordings, B000LE1GYE.

Greenwood, Lee. "God Bless the USA." *You've Got a Good Love Comin*. Ⓟ 1984 MCA Records, B000PLCMQE.

The Band. "The Weight." *Music from Big Pink*. Ⓟ 1968 Capitol Records, B00004YL5D.

Earle, Steve. "Jerusalem." *Jerusalem*. Ⓟ 2002 Artemis Records, B00006GEX6.

The Beatles. "Yesterday." *Help!* Ⓟ 1965 Capitol Records.

Caesar, Shirley. "Gotta Serve Somebody," written by Bob Dylan. *Gotta Serve Somebody: The Gospel Songs of Bob Dylan*. Ⓟ 2003 Sony Records, B00008NGAJ.

Jackson 5. "ABC." *ABC*. Ⓟ 1970 Motown Records.

Diamond, Neil. "Sweet Caroline." *Brother Love's Traveling Salvation Show*. Ⓟ 1990 MCA Records, B000002PBD.

Springsteen, Bruce. "Jesus Was an Only Son." *Devils & Dust*. Ⓟ 2005 Sony Records, B0007WF1WS.

## HOPE

Mann, Aimee. "Save Me." *A Little Happiness*. Ⓟ 2010 SideTracked Records, B003RWSCHG.

The Killers. "All These Things That I've Done." *Hot Fuss*. Ⓟ 2004 Island Records, B0002858YS.

The Replacements. "Here Comes a Regular." *Tim*. Ⓟ 1985 Sire/London/Rhino Records, B000002L8C.

West, Kanye. "Jesus Walks." *College Dropout*. Ⓟ 2004 Roc-a-Fella Records, B0001AP12G.

Smith, Elliott. "Miss Misery." *New Moon*. Ⓟ 2007 Kill Rock Stars Records, B000OMD4BG.

Radiohead. "Paranoid Android." *OK Computer.* ℗ 1997 Capitol Records, B000002UJQ.

Stevens, Sufjan. "Casimir Pulaski Day." *Illinois.* ℗ 2005 Asthmatic Kitty Records, B0009R1T7M.

Lennon, John. "Imagine." *Imagine.* ℗ 1971 Capitol Records, B003Y8YXFS.

U2. "All Because of You." *How to Dismantle an Atomic Bomb.* ℗ 2004 Interscope Records, B0006399FS.

Waits, Tom. "Jesus Gonna Be Here." *Bone Machine.* ℗ 1992 Island Records, B000001DVZ.

———. "Day after Tomorrow." *Real Gone.* ℗ 2004 Anti Records, B0002SDKG6.

Cohen, Leonard. "If It Be Your Will." *Various Positions.* ℗ 1984 Sony Music Entertainment.

———. "The Stranger Song." *Songs of Leonard Cohen.* ℗ 1967 Columbia Records.

## LOVE

Gaye, Marvin. "God Is Love." *What's Going On.* ℗ 1971 Motown Records, B0000060NF.

Over the Rhine. "Born." *Drunkards Prayer.* ℗ 2005 Back Porch Music, B0007QCLPY.

Death Cab for Cutie. "Title and Registration." *Transatlanticism.* ℗ 2003 Barsuk Records, B0000D1FDI.

John Doe (with Jane Wiedlin). "Forever for You." *Dim Stars, Bright Sky.* ℗ 2002 Reincarnate Music Records, B00006H692.

Coldplay. "X&Y." *X&Y.* ℗ 2005 Capitol Records, B0006L16N8.

John, Elton. "Tiny Dancer." *Mad Man across the Water.* ℗ 1971 This Record Company Ltd., B000001EGC.

Snow Patrol. "Run." *Final Straw.* ℗ 2004 A&M/Interscope Records.

Beck. "Everybody's Gotta Learn Sometimes." Cover of "Everybody's Got to Learn Sometime," by The Korgis. *Eternal Sunshine of the Spotless Mind.* ℗ 2004 Hollywood Records, B0001IXU1W.

Steam. "Na Na Hey Hey Kiss Him Goodbye." *Steam.* ℗ 1969 Mercury Records.

Madonna. "Live to Tell." *True Blue.* ℗ 1986 Warner Bros./WEA Records, B00005J6T0.

The Clash. "London Calling." *London Calling.* ℗ 1980 Epic Records, B00004BZ0N.

The Hold Steady. "How a Resurrection Really Feels." *Separation Sunday.* ℗ 2005 French Kiss Records, B0008KLW2C.

Stevens, Cat. "How Can I Tell You?" *Teaser and the Firecat.* ℗ 1971 A&M/Island Records, B00004T9W4.

Grateful Dead. "Friend of the Devil." *American Beauty.* ℗ 1970 Warner Bros., B00007LTIL.

# Index of Artists and Subjects